Transformed from Pain to Purpose

TACONDRA L. BROWN

Copyright

Table of Contents

Acknowledgements

ACKNOWLEDGEMENTS

Heavenly Father: Thank you for loving me so much that you gave your only Son to die for my sins. Thank you for knowing my worth and reminding me that I am yours. Thank you for the gift of salvation, I understand that this gift is not something I deserved or earned and I am forever grateful. Thank you for forgiving me and washing me clean of past sins, guilt, and shame. Thank you for setting me free from bondage and for being the platform on which I stand to share the message you have given me.

To My Husband: Eric, words alone cannot explain the love I have for you. You loved me years before we said, "I do". And even though you weren't always sure of how to love me, you still chose to. When I felt undeserving of your love you showed me just how much I was worth it. Thank you for keeping me grounded and for not giving up on me when I was ready to give up on myself. Words alone cannot express how grateful I am for you. I now love you from a different space within me, a space that I once denied you access to because resentment and bitterness dwelt there. You loved me through my brokenness, you supported me through my mess, gave me the liberty to be who I was, and allowed me to grow through the process of becoming who God has called me to be.

Thank you for believing in me. Although, my story does not paint the ideal image of you or me, I appreciate your boldness in allowing me to freely express my truths instead of worrying about protecting the image others may have of you. You've embarked along this journey of transparency with me and together we will share our story and message all over the world for God's glory. Our union is promised and purposed by God, a purpose that is still unraveling and I look forward to the full manifestation of it. I am committed to being your wife, lover, helpmeet, best friend, and partner till death do us part. Thank you for loving me at my worst and for this I want to give you all of me at my best.

To My Daughter Amiyah: There are many women in this world who can't and won't ever physically birth a child. I am more than grateful to God for allowing me to carry and give birth to you. Although, you don't remember being inside my womb, you are the only human being who has dwelled closest to my heart and knows a part of me that nobody else will ever understand. Thank you for encouraging me, for allowing me to take time away throughout this process, for being understanding and telling me to write freely about my experience so that someone else can relate.

I pray that your heart remains guarded as we discussed, and that you will take captive every thought that the enemy may try to place in your mind concerning anything mentioned in this book about your life. Rest assured knowing these things: I want you, I love you and I'll always be there for you. You are God's most precious gift to me and the best thing that I'll ever birth. You are my motivation and the reason why I could never give up on myself. Thank you for loving me unconditionally.

ACKNOWLEDGEMENTS

To my family and true friends: Thank you for encouraging me, motivating me, and believing in me when I didn't believe in myself. Thank you, mom and dad, for being transparent with me and allowing me to share details that have shaped me into the person I am today. You both encouraged me and supported me through the toughest of times. Not only have you watched me grow, but you accepted the challenge to pursue personal and spiritual growth yourselves. I'm proud to have you both as my parents. To my sisters, thank you for investing in me and for valuing the gift in me. I appreciate your loyalty to the woman I was and to the woman of God I am becoming. I love you all dearly. A special thanks to the spiritual midwives God placed in my life for the birthing of this book. I'm extremely grateful for the divine connections made throughout my journey.

Foreword

To my loving wife, thank you for being my rock, my lover, my friend, and my inspiration. Your anointing is undeniable, and this is just the beginning of what God has in store for you and us as a family. You have been beautifully transformed by the power and grace of God! Now it's time for you to help others on their journey.

Over a year ago you embarked on a journey I always knew you were prepared for. It was your time to confront your past with exposure, transparency, and forgiveness. We always hear people say God has a plan and He's always in control but often it falls on deaf ears because we don't understand it or accept it. I now know without a shadow of doubt that God truly does have a plan and He is always in control, because without Him nothing would be possible.

During the birthing of this book, my wife and I had to deal with the root of our issues both individually and together. Dealing with the pain of loss, isn't the easiest but with God's strength we overcame. So, if you're reading this book and you're seeking physical healing, an emotional breakthrough, or an encounter with the power of God then keep reading because this is the start of your beautiful transformation.

God Bless,
Eric

Introduction

It's amazing that I'm even writing this book. Years ago, God revealed to me in a dream that I would write a book about personal and spiritual growth. The book became a best-seller and I was extremely overwhelmed by the responses I received. I remember waking up in tears because it felt so real. I journaled and shared my heart on paper over the years, but didn't think anything of it. Fast forward a few more years and here I am writing my heart out on these pages. Little did I know that my life would be the research upon which this book would be written.

What qualifies me to write a book about my life? There's absolutely nothing spectacular or even halfway exciting about being me! Why on earth would anyone want to read a story about me or hear what I have to say when there are so many other people in this world who have something so much better to say? I'll be honest, I'd much rather write about someone else's life than my own and I'm not even a great writer! My writing is average at best and even though I'm a college graduate, I'm still a country girl at heart who stumbles over words.

The truth is, I don't always have organized thoughts or use the correct grammar, my range of vocabulary isn't all that broad and I'm really not a good speller, let alone speaker! I guess that's exactly why God used me to write this book. You see, my story isn't really about me, it is about a Savior, a Healer, a Transformer and a Restorer. It's all about HIM (Jesus) and how He beautifully transformed my life.

In life, we all experience some kind of loss at one point or another, whether it's the death of a loved one, heartache from a devastating break-up or divorce, a job loss, lifelong injuries, unfavorable conditions, or events that cause damage and hurt you.

Perhaps, like me you have suffered a loss that changed you forever or maybe you will. I know firsthand what it feels like to experience joy and pain on the same day. Giving birth to my beautiful daughter years ago brought me so much joy, but who knew that waking up barren hours later would bring me so much pain. Pain that I would allow to define my worth, become my disability, and my comfort zone.

The pain runs deep and you question God "Why?" "Why me?" "What did I do to deserve this?" I hear you asking, "Why does God allow bad things to happen to good people?" I've asked this same question time and time again. "God, why would you take my womb? Why would you allow me to suffer and go through so much pain? I'm a good person! What did I do to deserve this?" Have you ever felt angry with God for something bad that happened to you? For someone evil harming and causing you pain? Have you felt abandoned, rejected, and forsaken after a loss? Maybe you've allowed the circumstances surrounding your loss to define your worth, who you are, what you can do, and who you will become. Sometimes, it's just easier for us to accept defeat, settle for less, embrace our fate, and soak in complacency and fear, rather than choosing to rise above our struggles and let go of the negative things that has defined us for so long.

Many people aren't willing or vulnerable enough to share their loss and the pain they silently suffer from because it's uncomfortable to talk about it. However, the last time I checked, being bound doesn't feel all that great either. It's heart breaking to see people longing to be set free, but not realizing that they're bound to themselves. Are you one of those people? I was.

My question to you is what are you waiting for? Are you waiting for someone to apologize for the pain you've suffered before you choose to forgive and let go? Are you waiting for life to make all the wrongs, right? Do you believe God owes you something for what you've gone through? Beloved, I'm sorry but it doesn't work that way. Trust me, I know. When you become desperate for your freedom as much as you are for your next breath, you will give up your right to be angry and embrace a life of healing and forgiveness.

What if I told you that everything that has happened in your life, whether good or bad, is no misprint. That every loss you've endured and every circumstance you'll encounter, fashions the person you are meant to become? Would you believe me? I know, I wouldn't believe me either. But it's true. Regardless of what you've been through or what you will go through, there is always a reason and a purpose for it. The things we go through prepares us for a purpose greater than ourselves. We must realize that God doesn't always orchestrate the bad in our lives, but He knows how to take the negatives and turn them into positives if you let Him.

If you've never been told this before, let me be the first to tell you. Beloved, you are valued, you are loved, you are wanted, you are worthy, and you are not forsaken! The feeling of abandonment and rejection are fabricated by the enemy because he wants to abort the power, the purpose, and the dreams that God has placed inside of you. The bible tells us that "the adversary walks around like a roaring lion, seeking whom he may devour (1 Peter 5:8)." The devil is after your purpose, your marriage, God-ordained relationships, your gifts, and anything else because if he can destroy it, he knows that he'll put a stop to you and the lives you are meant to reach for Christ. Don't let the enemy rob you of your joy, silence you and keep you bound with feelings of inadequacy and hopelessness. Don't give him the position or power to rule over your life!

You are not alone! There are many people like you and I who have suffered long enough from something that no one else knows about. Do not allow the dark cloud of guilt and shame to linger over you anymore. You may not understand it right now, but someone's deliverance, healing, growth, and life depends on the message that God has given you. YOU are a book worth reading! Even if the pages of your story are still being written, God can and will use you where you are NOW! Your shortcomings and mistakes qualifies you for His call! Hence, the reason I can no longer be invisible or silent; shying away from who I am, what I've done, and what makes me different.

The cost of trust is transparency and I am aware of the risks associated with exposure. Some people will pass judgement, others may have something negative to say, and then there are those who will take what they read and create their own stories. I pray that people be blessed by the words penned in this book and I understand that not everyone will be encouraged by my story or transformation. There will always be tares among the wheat and I thank God for delivering me from people and their dark opinions. Increasing value in your life is priceless, compared to the cost of protecting a reputation I don't possess. If anything, the heart and character of who I am versus who people think I should be will be revealed through this book. Allowing God to shine light into the dark, forbidden places of my heart was not easy nor comfortable, but it was necessary. God certainly did reconstructive surgery and He took out my heart of stone and replaced it with a heart of flesh (Ezekiel 36:26). My prayer is that your heart will be open and as fertile soil, ready to receive the seed. That seed is the transforming Word of God.

Because I am human, you may come across typos in this book or even find yourself getting bored reading at some points. Just stop, take a break, put the book down and don't forget to pick it back up later! Read this book at your own pace. I did my best to keep your attention and to keep you somewhat entertained without crying the whole time (hopefully). You will cry! You might even get mad or offended, you may have some thoughts and questions about me, my family, husband, or even yourself as you read this book. It's okay! That's normal! Write them down and ask me later! You might get an answer from me, you might not, depending on the question! No matter what, I just want you to enjoy this journey with me.

I pray that my story adds value to your life, provide you with insight about your own pain, help you to gain new perspective, reveal the beauty of your brokenness, and birth healing, transformation, and restoration. By the end of this book you will be inspired to transform beautifully and help someone else do the same! Are you ready? Because God is ready to transform your pain into purpose! Let's Go!

Who I Am

I was born and raised in a small town right outside of Plant City, FL called Beallsville, 'The Country' is what we called it. A community where everybody knows each other, are related, or feel like family to you. My wonderful parents, Vincent and Juana Wright, raised all five of us in a three-bedroom, two-bathroom, single-wide trailer that sat on land surrounded by dirt roads, strawberry fields, trees, and cows.

There is my oldest brother, Javarious (Jay), my brother Vincent Jr. (lil' Vint), my twin sister, Tacara (Cara), my baby sister, Vinterica and me. Both of my brothers are from prior relationships my parents were involved in. My mom's son, Jay, is the cherished firstborn. He's the first grandson, was the admired football and basketball star, and was also the first "rebellious" one. He has a heart of gold, but can catch an attitude worse than a female sometimes! Just kidding.(Not really). My father's son, Lil' Vint is a year younger than Jay. He didn't live with us permanently, but spent most of the weekends and sometimes longer with us. I don't remember Lil Vint being involved in sports, but I do know that he liked staying in the room by himself playing video games. Similar to me, he was the quiet and reserved brother.

Together, my parents had three girls. My baby sister Vinterica was born eight years after me and Cara. I have sweet memories of helping care for my baby sister, but most of my sweetest childhood memories are with my twin.

The ones I remember most were created right in our front yard. The yard was long and wide like an Olympics gymnastics floor. Okay, so maybe it wasn't that big in real life but, it was huge to me. A wood beam sat on the lawn where our parents would park their cars and Cara and I would take turns creating beam routines, while pretending to be our favorite gymnast, Dominique Dawes. Dominique would use the entire length of the beam during her routine and performed a mount to start the routine and a dismount to finish it. We watched her confidently showcase her skills on both the beam and floor routine with beauty and grace. She made it look so easy that we believed we could do it too! We performed leaps, jumps, twists, high and low leg turns all over that wood beam. We imagined ourselves doing flips, handsprings, and other acrobatic moves that our bodies wouldn't completely allow us to do before executing our pretend dismounts.

We ran from one corner of the lawn to the other doing more cartwheels, round-offs, imaginary flips, and whatever other floor exercises we could make up along the way. When gymnastics playtime was over we would grab our bicycles, lay them sideways on the ground and imagine we were school bus drivers. We positioned the front tire ahead of us and used it as the steering wheel and the bike stand was used to open and close the bus door. Right before it was time to go inside and get ready for dinner we would lay beside one another in the grass, exhausted of energy, and gaze into the sky looking for hearts, rabbits, horses, faces, angels, Jesus, and other things our vast imaginations believed were embedded in the clouds. Oh, how I miss those days.

Most of our time was spent at the youth recreational center in our community. We called it the 'U-Center' because we really thought it was called that. Sometimes, our dad would come home from work and yell, "Cara and Condra! Let's go!" We'd walk to the park to watch him play baseball or basketball with his buddies. Our journey to and from the park involved us walking a million-miles-per hour just to keep up with daddy's long strides. For some reason, the night time sky always graciously appeared when we were still out, forcing us to walk down the pitch-dark road on our way home. Talk about something scary!

During the summer, we practically lived at the U-center with all the other kids who had nothing exciting to do. We enjoyed all of the activities, arts and crafts, playing pool table, video games, and board games. Baking in the sun and drowning in humidity is not my cup of tea, but I still enjoyed going outside playing tether ball, red-light green-light, Mother-May-I, and flying high on the swings. The highlight of my day at the center was snack time! A carton of grape juice and a chocolate chip cookie made those long summer days at the U-center so worth it!

Cara is the oldest twin by approximately two minutes but of course, I act like the oldest. Actually, I would have been the oldest if she didn't bump me out of the way as we were exiting the birth canal. As our mom was giving birth to us the doctors yelled, "Baby A has just crossed over Baby B!" Which resulted in her having an emergency C-section that led to Cara snatching my birthright. Cara was technically the middle child after our baby sister was born, but I always felt like the one in the middle. Being the middle child is usually associated with feeling different and lonely most of the time. Sometimes I felt out of place in my own family; as if I didn't fit in. Perhaps, not wanting to "blend in" or do the things everyone else wanted to do left me with the impression that I was different. When everyone else wanted to hang out as a family, I preferred staying home, cuddling with my cats, or playing music. Having a twin sister kept me from being alone, however, it didn't stop the feelings of loneliness. I coped with my lonesomeness by expressing myself through journaling, writing poetry, listening to music and playing piano. Whenever I needed an outlet, I would walk next door to my grandmother's house, sit down in front of her beautiful, tan colored piano and play my little heart out. I often heard songs on the radio or in my head and tried my best to play them. I was very much in tune with myself as a child, even though I'd later question who I was as a young adult. As I look back now, I can see how being different also made me the strongest among my siblings. Now that we're older, I've become the voice of reason for my family, they look up to me more than I imagined they ever would.

Being a Twin

I'm fortunate enough to have shared a womb and a bedroom with my first "best friend" until we were about 14 years old. The bond my twin sister and I have is special. I know that if no one else ever understands me or my heart, she will. We share the same DNA, so she has to understand me, right? Though we are alike in many ways, our differences make us incredibly unique. Most identical twins are extremely close; they look exactly alike, dress alike, sound alike, walk alike, live alike, do everything together, and basically can't live without each other- at least, that's the what most people imagine being a twin is like. It's also the way our dad and his twin brother were raised, yes my dad is an identical twin who had identical twins!

When we were little girls Cara and I looked and dressed very much alike. But as we got older, we appeared to look more like sisters than twins. Some people even question to this day if we're identical. People can easily tell us apart by the difference in our faces. I have moles on my face, she doesn't; Cara has a gap in between her teeth, I don't; her face is fuller than mine, but my nose is shaped a little different than hers. I've always been a few pounds lighter than her, although, she has always been more athletic than me. Crazy, right? Softball is the only sport we didn't mind going outside and getting dirty for back in the day and to this day we both still enjoy playing the sport. Our style of dressing is also different, I prefer quality whereas she prefers quantity. I favor a classy, girl-next-door type of style with a pinch of sophistication and elegance, whereas Cara favors a more relaxed, casual, tomboy-style every now and then. On the other hand, she is more daring than I am and won't hesitate to step out into something short and sexy.

I like to imagine that we are each other's alter ego. She's literally night and I'm day! (Do you get it? Darkness versus light?) Okay, let me explain. Growing up, I was often called the "good" twin and she was labeled the "bad" twin. At least that's what some people thought. One may think that the title given would be helpful and not harmful but the truth is, that very title placed unwanted pressure on me and birthed the indication of me being perfect in my mind. I made every effort to live up to being the "good twin" and with that came loads of burdens. I'll explain more later in this book.

Cara and I both have similar personality traits. We are both introverts by nature, but know how to be extroverts when necessary. Our differences have always made us slightly feel worlds apart. When we were in elementary school our mom made the decision to separate us from each other. From that period on and throughout high school we didn't have any of the same classes, except for maybe homeroom class and a few electives. Splitting us up in elementary school was a big deal back then, there was even a newspaper article about it. The reason for her separating us was often questioned, but she meant no harm. She wanted us to soar without having to depend on each other and to establish our own individualities. My mom explained to me that after seeing my dad and his twin brother struggle to live lives independent of each other she decided she didn't want her twin girls to be that way. Now that I'm older, I can appreciate her decision, though I would have enjoyed being around my sister more in school back then. The benefit is that my identity isn't wrapped up in my sister nor is her identity wrapped up in me. We are who we are and we're okay with that. A more difficult issue was finding the balance between the two sides that makes me who I am.

A Perfect Mixture of The Two

There are two sides to who I am and who you are too. God knew the precise formula to fashion me for His purpose. I'm thankful for my earthly father and anyone that knows me knows it's no secret that I'm a daddy's girl. If you place a wig on him you'd probably think he was the one who gave birth to me! Growing up, I imagined my dad being a decorated man of prestige, a clean, suit-wearing businessman, or a prolific speaker.

For one, I thought that would mean I'd be a little more "bright" or have the ability to articulate my words better if I were graced with those genes, but also because society paints the picture that those type of men are the most powerful, influential, and well-respected. Well, that's not who my dad is, but I certainly do have the upmost respect and admiration for him. Instead, he is the best pancake-making, hamburger-flipping, loud, humorous, t-shirt and jean wearing, hard-working electrician and handy-man I know! He's not afraid to get his hands dirty and he can fix almost anything! Electrical work is his passion and is something he was introduced to by his father at a young age. Oh, and he loves fishing!

The only time I remember my daddy missing a day of work was if he was sick, hurt, or going fishing! Plenty of days he'd come home from his job, take a quick nap, and go right back out in the community to do more work. His work ethic has remained the same over the years and I find it admirable. I endeavored to one day have a man with superb work ethics like him. The relationship I have with my dad is special. I clearly remember in my crawling days, sitting and watching Barney on the television, while waiting for him to get home from work. He'd open the front door and scream "arrgghhh!" to scare us, then chase us down the hallway crawling on his knees. I vividly remember mornings before school when Daddy would make us huge, thin pancakes drenched in butter for Cara and me to share. The edges were crisped to perfection. He usually took us on fun fishing trips and whenever he left without us I would eagerly await his return. I got excited about seeing the size and amount of fish he caught and took delight in watching him scale them with a fork and filet them with his knife. Mama got excited too and she'd run to the stove and fry those bad boys up! We kept a freezer full of fresh fish!

My daddy is the laid-back, down-to-earth parent. He's always been more of a friend than a parent, which wasn't a terrible thing for us, but for him not so much. He threatened to be stricter with us at times, but we never took him seriously. When Cara and I would get into fights, mama would send him into our room with a belt to discipline us. Instead of whipping us, he'd talk to us, make us hug each other, then make us promise to tell mama that he whooped us! On the other hand, mama was the authoritative parent, although she had permissive tendencies. She wouldn't take any mess from us and didn't hesitate to pop us in the mouth, throw a broom, remote control, or whatever else she could find to knock us out if we were being rebellious. From childhood to adulthood, the close-knit bond between my father and I has never been broken. In fact, it's only grown stronger. He was my first hero and in my eyes, he could do no wrong.

I may be a daddy's girl at heart, but I am totally my mother's child! Juana, Juana, do what she wanna! (Inside joke). My mother has a beautiful spirit, she is loving, warmhearted, selfless, caring, considerate, and very respectable. She'll do anything in her power to help her family and anyone she comes in contact with. Yet again, she has the tough exterior, she is a woman warrior. One that loves hard like a mama bear and is very protective and territorial. I've always admired her authenticity, she is praised for her genuine nature and she is not the one to bite her tongue about anything. She doesn't believe in sugar coating the truth and if for some reason she tries to keep silent, the look on her face usually reveals that there is a problem. I am just like her and God is still working on delivering us both in that department! She truly has the genuine spirit of her mother and the strong nature of her father, the ideal blend of the two.

Mama never really had a set occupation from what I can remember, but she certainly had her share of jobs. She pretty much worked whenever she wanted to and my daddy never had a problem with it. If you know me personally or if I have ever shared my résumés with you, you're probably laughing at this point. My mom worked as a teacher in daycares, a phlebotomist, a registrar at the hospital and the community college, a secretary/case manager at the health department, a juvenile detention officer, and quite a few other positions. I'm not even going to think about listing the jobs I've worked! From my point of view, my mom likes to explore her options! Okay, so maybe she was really just trying to discover her purpose, but at least she wasn't afraid to try new things! Yes, I'm defending her and myself too! I'm sure you know what it's like jumping from one opportunity to the next in search of fulfillment, purpose or just better pay, right? Don't act like you haven't done it!

If a position wasn't the right fit or if the job caused too much stress, she had no problem walking away from it. Neither do I! She told me about a time she left a job during her lunch break and laughed the entire way home because she knew she wasn't going back! It cracked me up because I could totally see myself doing that! Again, I am my mother's child. I actually enjoyed having my mother at home. Sometimes, we'd come home from school and go do aerobics with her at the U-center, but she made sure that dinner was prepared and the house was all clean and comfy first. Mama did everything for us: washed, ironed, and folded all of our clothing, attended all of my music concerts and events that mattered the most in school. I adored her being available whenever we needed her. Seeing how my mom nurtured and cared for us and our home greatly influenced the woman I am today. I prefer to be the stay-at-home-wife who sees the hubby and kid off to school, runs errands all day, manages the calendar, cleans, cooks, and sets the environment in the home. But then again, with the good always comes the bad. My relationship with my mom has always been different compared to the relationship I have with my dad. As a teen, I sensed a slight disconnection and discerned that she had some resentment towards our dad and the way we viewed him. It wasn't until I wrote this book that I discovered the disconnect was rooted in deeper issues regarding my father that I won't bother going into, but it involved her protecting our image of him.

My mother's desire to protect her family made her appear to be the difficult wife and parent at times. Show me what looks like perfection from the ground up and I'll show you the damaged roots that exist from the ground down. There is no such thing as a perfect person, parent, a perfect marriage, or even a perfect family. We all have secrets and issues that occur in life that leave us scarred. You may have been reading this and thought that we had the perfect family but there were times when our "peaceful home" wasn't so peaceful. My parents often got into verbal and physical fights with each other. My ears became immune to the loud thuds of wrestling and rumbling, the uproars of arguing back and forth was terrifying at times.

Deep inside, I knew my parents loved each other, but I couldn't understand why they would inflict pain on each other. I wanted to believe that I wasn't affected by the exposure to such an environment, but just as sure as time supposedly heals all wounds time certainly reveals all wounds as well.

I look at my life now compared to my mother's and I see some similarities. I'm grateful for the vulnerable conversations with my family about the environments I was exposed to back then because it helped me connect certain dots and relieved me of the pressures and insecurities I've struggled with as an adult. I'll dig a little deeper into my family history to explain.

My Paternal Side

My dad is the baby boy of eight siblings on his side of the family. The Wright's. His mother, Audrey, my grandmother, was the sweetest, church-going, strawberry-jam making, pea-shelling, beautician in our community who touched everybody's head at some point. She was a selfless person, always willing to reach into her purse, or bosom, to place money in someone else's hand. She would give you the clothes off of her back if you needed it. She was not perfect, by far, but she was a nurturer, encourager, friend, and grandma. I spent a lot of time with her as a child, considering we lived right next door to her and my granddaddy.

My dad's father Arthur, was a well-known, reserved, hard-working, disciplinarian whose sole purpose was to provide for his family from my view. Granddaddy would find little moments to play with us when we were little babies and toddlers, but it seemed like the older we got the more distant he became. He never missed a high school or college graduation though. For me, his detached demeanor made him unapproachable sometimes, I would easily go and ask my grandma for something before I went to him.

My dad inherited his hard-working trait from his father and by the grace of God, he is much more approachable. Most of my father's older siblings are well-educated and successful from my stance. My aunts and uncles raised their kids in communities filled with huge, beautiful homes, private schools, and what looked like civilized neighbors. I enjoyed visiting their homes as a kid. They had plenty space for us to play in, a bunch of activities to enjoy, and my cousins had their own bedrooms! At that age, I didn't understand why they had so much more than us and why their lifestyle looked different from ours. Sometimes I wished I could be them or at least live with them for a while. Don't get me wrong, I was thankful for our comfy, single-wide trailer and the things my parents gave us. Christmas and birthdays were always pleasant and filled with gifts, fun times, and smiles. I would have never known if my parents struggled financially. Undeniably, I still questioned why our lifestyle didn't look like that of my aunts, uncles, and cousins.

Fast forward to now and I see things differently. Before my grandma Audrey passed away I spent some much-needed time with her in the hospital. Even in her last days she still maintained a giving spirit, she gave unselfishly and on a few occasions, she tried to pay the nurses for bringing her food she refused to eat. I ordered dinner from the café for her one day: Blackened salmon, broccoli, and a sweet potato. She took a few bites, but didn't want to finish it and told me and Eric to eat the food instead. We politely declined, but she insisted and said she wouldn't eat another meal while in that hospital if we didn't eat it. Needless to say, we ate everything left on the plate. The look on her face was priceless as she watched us shove food down our mouth like it was our last meal. When I look at myself in the mirror I often see her reflection, a heart that desires to feed and help other people, sometimes at my own expense.

Grandma was extremely proud of our family accomplishments and she expressed her deepest love for her children. "It's so many of y'all grands and great grands," she exclaimed with a toothy smile. After staring blankly at the wall or TV for a few minutes she'd then say, "You know I have a bunch of educated fools! I don't know why some of them act the way they do." She giggled. I heard her say this a few times, but I examined her body language after saying it too. A dispirited countenance fell upon her face each time she uttered those words, a sorrowful look of guilt and a lack of understanding appeared.

It's normal for families to have disputes and disagreements, but what we sometimes fail to realize is regardless of our differences, bickering, tension, and hearts filled with resentment leads to division and blemishes a family legacy. This side of my family greatly influenced my desire to live a better lifestyle as an adult but a harsh reality I observed is, though being educated and pursuing wealth can afford you pleasant things in life it can't guarantee you happiness, peace, or love. At the end of the day, love is all we have. It's not something that can be bought and there's no amount of money, possessions, or accomplishments that are worth the price of peace and love with the ones who matter the most.

My Maternal Side

I battled with fully embracing the other side of who I am because I struggled to fit in. My mom is the second oldest of five siblings. Elizabeth Broadnax, my grandmother, is still the most beautiful, soft spoken, humble, and kind-hearted spirit walking this earth. She truly has the heart of Jesus. She probably won't agree, but from my view she is a ride or die saint and has been since the day she was born! Okay, so I may be over exaggerating a little, but she's my grandma and this is my book.

Now my pop, Roosevelt Broadnax, was a pipe-smoking, unsanctified-cussing, liquor-drinking, undercover gentle giant who didn't play about his woman, children, nor family. He was a protector, he loved hard and would do anything for you, but he didn't mind telling you like it was either. These two earthly beings were like night and day; holy and unholy. The bond they shared clearly illustrates the scripture in the bible that speaks of the unsanctified husband being made holy by his wife (1 Corinthians 7:4).

They are one of the reasons I know for a fact that God has a sense of humor. Grandma and Pop were the most unequally yoked personalities God could have ever joined together to create a miracle of love. They were joined together in holy matrimony for almost fifty years before pop passed away and I must admit that their love story is unique and amazingly beautiful. Accolades and material wealth isn't prevalent on this side of my family, but there is an abundance of love.

Cara and I spent the majority of our time with cousins on our mother's side of the family. We all attended the same schools, lived in the same neighborhood, attended the same church, enjoyed birthdays together, fought each other, made each other cry, and did all the other normal things first cousins do. Cara connected more with our cousins on this side, whereas I related more with our cousins on my dad's side. I felt like a 'fish out of water' on this side of the family, desperate to fit in and feel accepted. I wasn't treated horribly or made great fun of, but I was often labeled the "white girl" because I exercised good grammar, excelled in school, and displayed good conduct.

I was labeled as the scary cat, the one who avoided trouble. No matter how much I tried to look like them or alter my behavior to blend in they'd say, "Condra, you ain't gonna do this" or that. "Just stop, cause you don't even look right!" They insisted. When I stopped to think about it, they were right. Trying to be someone you're not is way more complicated than simply being the person that God created you to be. If I had a dollar for every moment I wasted trying to be who I thought people wanted me to be, I would probably be a millionaire by now. I wish I could go back in time and have a conversation with the younger version of myself. I'd reassure her that it's okay to be different because God didn't create one person to be the same. I'd encourage her to boldly stand out and not worry about trying to blend in. I would advise her to dig for the treasures within, cultivate the gifts and talents God placed inside of her, seek God's love, approval, and affirmation and not to lose sight of herself trying to win the approval of mere humans. I knew my cousins loved me and would fight for me if I ever needed them to, but I wanted more than their company and protection back then. I wanted something that could only be given by God.

Can you relate? Did you ever struggle with being different and finding balance between the two sides of who you are? Did you look for acceptance and validation in all of the wrong places? Perhaps, there was an individual in your family who helped influence your heart and brought balance to your life at a young age? For me, that person was my Aunt Sheryll, she was married to my mother's oldest brother. She's a beautiful, God-fearing, well-spoken, educated, fashionista from the Bahamas. Auntie could come across a bit intimidating because of her powerful presence and strict demeanor, but I adored being in her presence.

Unlike most of my cousins, I was the one who jumped at the opportunity to go places with auntie and grandma Liz (because they were a package deal) even though we usually ended up somewhere that involved church a great deal of the time! Auntie was the youth leader at our church and she laid the biblical foundation, and instilled godly principles and values in all of us.

I spent numerous Sunday afternoons at her house watching videos about the bible and learning about Jesus. One reason I loved spending time with auntie was because I knew if we went off somewhere it was guaranteed that we'd do one thing, EAT! As long as there was food involved, your girl was down for whatever! I'd beg to go home with auntie after church on Sundays because she would let me help prepare dinner. My favorite thing to do was fry cornbread on top of the stove that looked like pancakes and make the orange, fruit-flavored drink, called Tang. We always prepared a salad to go with our meals, even though I was not a fan of rabbit food back then. After setting the table in the dining room, Auntie would go to my Uncle's mancave and serve him dinner, then the rest of us would gather together to say grace and eat.

There were many factors that drew me to aunt Sheryll. For one, she kept a closet full of classy clothing, the cutest high-heels, boots, and other shoes I longed to dress up in. She even had a vanity in her master bathroom covered with makeup, brushes, perfumes and little goodies that I secretly covered myself in when I snuck into her room. On a more serious note, I found pleasure in the tone she set in her home. The atmosphere was welcoming, peaceful, comfortable, clean, and extremely relaxing. I also admired the effort she put into ensuring that the relationships with her family, children, God-children, nieces and nephews were secure. Her parenting style was attractive, she enforced rules and gave consequences for not following them. She always explained the reasons behind her rules and if she had to discipline us, she never hesitated to love on us afterwards. I now realize that auntie offered something I felt was lacking in my own home back then, structure. My parents provided structure, but only to a certain extent. Daily routines weren't consistent and they didn't always enforce rules or habits, like making sure we brushed our teeth twice a day, eating healthy, or exercising. If we brushed our teeth in the morning, didn't starve, and at least moved at some point during the day then we were good! Really though!

Thankfully, I don't remember getting spankings from aunt Sheryll as often as some of my cousins did. I was very obedient when it came to her and every time she opened her mouth to speak I felt like a little kid, sitting Indian-style at her feet, soaking in every word. To this day I feel the same way when she pours wisdom into me. I know she isn't perfect but, I think highly of my aunt. I love and respect her for being the person who made me feel okay with being the different one in a family that I felt slightly disconnected from. She stood out to me and didn't look or act like anyone else I knew on the Broadnax side of my family, but she loved us all the same. She was my middle ground, the central point of this invisible, see-saw like scale I used to balance one side of who I was to the other. She became my example and ensample of what a Godly woman and wife looked like. To this day, I admire everything about her. Her confidence, transparency, style, and conduct is something I emulate and model after in my own life. It's safe to say that I'm also a miniature version of her with a slight twist of Juana and my own unique self.

Product of Your Environment or Choices

History definitely has a way of repeating itself, but it doesn't mean you have to spend your life avoiding becoming a product of your DNA. I'll admit, there are some not-so-pretty behaviors, conditions, and struggles I am genetically predisposed to. Although we don't get to choose our biological family or the environments in which we are raised, there are things we have the power to change with our choices. I firmly believe that we are not just products of our environment but, our choices. I realized that I can't be disappointed about the family I was born into or the environments in which I was exposed because God knew exactly where I needed to be in addition to every detail, circumstance, or condition that was essential to fulfilling His purpose for my life.

Have you battled with trusting God in this area of your life? Have you ever felt hopeless in your environment or like the families you were born into was a huge mistake on God's part? Perhaps, you've blamed your current reality on the decisions and choices of someone else in your family? Once I stumbled across the profound truth and power that God gave us to make a choice, something clicked on the inside of me. Freewill can be used to our advantage or our demise. Your environments don't have to define who you are, who you become, or what you have the ability to do in life. You have the power of choice! You get to choose what good to take away from your upbringing and what bad to leave behind. You have the power to overcome every obstacle that has been set before you and reinvent the wheel for your life! It's up to YOU to make the choice! No one else can choose for you! Not having everything I wanted and not always being in the best environments as a child fostered humility and awakened a desire in me to want better, do better, and achieve more. With that, meant making a choice to go against "the norm of thinking" in my family. I had to change my mindset and that was one hundred percent of the struggle.

Strongholds, chains, and generational curses must be broken if you're going to make a difference in your life.

Strongholds and Generational Curses

Stronghold:

"A place where a particular cause or belief is strongly defended or upheld", "A fortified place; a place of security or survival."

Anything considered as a generational curse is primarily based on the religious teachings and concept that comes from God's Ten Commandments.

"You must not make for yourself an idol of any kind or an image of anything in the heavens or on the earth or in the sea. You must not bow down to them or worship them, for I, the LORD your God, am a jealous God who will not tolerate your affection for any other gods. I lay the sins of the parents upon their children; the entire family is affected—even children in the third and fourth generations of those who reject me." - Exodus 20: 4-5

I don't know what past iniquities my forefathers are guilty of, but I've certainly been handed my share of the punishment between both sides of my family. I recognize three strongholds and generational curses that run rampant in my life and family: laziness, fear, and a limited mentality. I know plenty of people, like me who have great potential, yet settle for less in life because they're too lazy or easily intimidated. Let's not forget those who are tired and overwhelmed by work. I mean, who doesn't physically enjoy being lazy every now and then? I certainly do! Nevertheless, laziness is a negative habit that is learned and when you fail to correct the behavior it becomes a mindset that's hard to break. The laziness I'm referring to is a way of thinking that prevented me from making moves to better myself. This way of thinking says that being stretched outside of your comfort zone, whether that is a geographical location, from people, a job, or a way of life is terrifying, painful, and impossible to do. Therefore, you never seize the opportunity to grow and encounter new experiences.

My Pop would often say that he was "waiting for his ship to come along." He used to dream about building a home large enough to accommodate the entire family. As a little girl, I never really understood what he meant by "waiting for his ship to come along" but I knew he played the lottery often. Perhaps, he was hoping to hit the jackpot one day to fulfill his dream? Unfortunately, that never happened. In no way am I stating that my pop was physically lazy, one thing he couldn't stand was a lazy man. But I'd like to examine the fruit that this mindset produced in me and from what I've observed in my own family.

Before I go any further, let me apologize to anyone reading this who might take offense; especially those related to me who might perceive this in a negative light. My objective is not to tear down anyone or anything except the mindset and strongholds that have kept me bound. I use to pray for God to make me rich so that I could afford nice things and help take care of my family, but when it came to putting in the work I was slothful. I'm not just talking about putting my hands to work, but my mind. I simply didn't want to do it because thinking sometimes is too much work! You're probably thinking I'm contradicting myself based on what you read earlier about my desire to achieve more in life. Well, my desire never changed but the determination and motivation to obtain more, that's a different story.

It seems like I spent most of my time struggling to find the "get-up-and-go" energy just to make things happen! I finally came to the realization that prosperity and wealth doesn't just fall out of the sky and into our laps. It's just NOT going to happen that way and if it does, chances are it won't last. Nothing in life is just handed to us, unless of course, you're born into a fortunate family or left with a hefty inheritance; definitely not my case.

Faith, goals, WORK, initiative, and efforts produce FRUIT, not dreams or fantasies! As I'm maturing spiritually, I'm learning that when you desire something in life you must go after it even though you will stumble along the way! The bible teaches us as believers to intentionally pursue Christ. I like the International Standard translation of Philippians 3:12 that says, "It's not that I have already reached this goal or have already become perfect. But I keep pursuing it, hoping somehow to embrace it just as I have been embraced by the Messiah Jesus." When a desire is placed inside of you by God it's up to you to capture that which has captured your heart. If you want to be wealthy in life, period, you have to put in work. If you want to live the abundant, prosperous life that Christ came and died for you to have then you must put in work! If you want a successful marriage guess what, YOU GOTTA PUT IN THE WORK! You only get out of life what you're willing to put into it. Not everyone is willing to admit it, but this restricted mentality of "waiting for a ship to come along" is one of the mindsets I identified in my life as a hindrance.

Mediocrity and complacency is infectious and limits the mind. Glancing over my family history, I find that the gifts and talents are many, but ambition, determination, and perseverance are few. Although I am a planner, failing to plan ahead for the future and being a good steward is another struggle I've battled with. I know the scripture tells us to live one day at a time and not to worry about tomorrow; for tomorrow will care for itself (Matthew 6:34). There's nothing wrong with believing and having faith that God will provide for us, however, Proverbs 13:16 says, "a wise man thinks ahead..." This lets me know that when you fail to plan or think ahead, you can plan on failing.

There are multiple stories and scriptures throughout the bible that teach us to be wise, good stewards over what we're given, and to plan for the future. In the book of Genesis, Pharaoh was warned to reserve a fifth of the produce of the land of Egypt in the seven years of abundance. His provisions prepared him for the seven years of famine that came thereafter. In Proverbs 6:6-8 we are advised to observe the behavior of the ant that "prepares her food in the summer and gathers her provision in the harvest." Yes, we depend on God to make provisions for all our needs, but it doesn't mean that we are exempt from planning ahead. Being a good steward over finances and the things God gave me period was another battle for me. It doesn't matter how much money you make or what possessions you acquire, if you never learn to manage and invest in what God gives you, it will cease to exist.

What strongholds and generational curses in your family can you identify that are holding you back from being the best version of yourself? I challenge you to ask questions, get answers, and be bold enough to declare that "enough is enough!" I chose to put an end to the strongholds and generational curses that bombarded my life and created a new path for my daughter. I will be the change for those in my family to see and inspire them to overcome! Perhaps, the change you want to see in your family must start with you.

Puppy Love

I don't remember the exact age I was when this skinny, chocolate boy, with a tail hanging from the back of his head, wearing braces and eye glasses came into my life. Meeting him was no mistake, it was indeed a divine connection. His family called him EJ but I preferred to call him by his name, Eric. Perhaps, it was because my favorite Disney movie, The Little Mermaid, featured a prince named Eric who had a dog named Max. In case you aren't familiar with the movie, it's about a mermaid named Ariel, who fell in love with a human and her desire to be with him was so great that she sold her voice to Ursula the witch of the sea, to become a human herself. With hopes that she could win the heart of the handsome prince she went out on a three-day mission to have him fall in love with her and kiss her so that she could remain a human forever.

If you're familiar with the movie, you would agree that Ariel was determined to go through hell and high waters just to be with the man she loved. She disobeyed her father, rebelled against the crab Sebastian and she went after her heart's desire instead of living up to everyone else's expectations of her. I could definitely relate to Ariel being the child who stood out, was gifted, desired to please everyone, but dared to live life on her own terms. Like Ariel, I was the one who could do no wrong or at least that's what people thought.

My mom and Eric's mom actually grew up together and are really good friends. Their parents also knew each other and both of our families attended the same church, our families are so close that we almost thought that we were related! Sometimes during the summer, Eric's mom would drop him and his sister off at our place while she went to work. Some mornings I'd wake up to find them standing over my bunk-bed, staring and waiting patiently for me and Cara to get up so we could all go outside. I didn't view Eric as anything more than a friend back then. In fact, I was more interested in his light-skinned cousin who attended the same church.

I'll never forget one sunny Sunday, April 24, 1994, it was our ninth birthday. We were in church and while the pastor was preaching, Eric's cousin and I were busy smiling and passing hints back and forth to each other about our secret crushes. I believe he wanted to ask me to be his girlfriend, but was too afraid to do so.

After church, all of our family and friends went with us to Lithia Springs Park to swim and enjoy a barbecue. The water at Lithia Springs was freezing cold, as always, and the weather was perfect. We danced, ate, opened gifts, and reveled in our birthday splendor. After everyone left the park a few people came by our house that evening to hang out. Eric, his cousin and a few of our female cousins were there as well. We were in my brother's room playing a video game and somehow my crazy cousin persuaded us to play a kissing game. I ended up having to kiss Eric and that small peck on his huge lips changed everything, it ignited something between us and my crush on his cousin became irrelevant.

This innocent puppy love between Eric and I was birthed and my twin sister and his cousin ended up taking their chance at puppy love. I guess you can say it all worked out for the best. Surprisingly,

Eric and I grew fonder of each other as the years went by. Our puppy love blossomed into a more meaningful relationship with struggles and all as we grew up into young adults. I became this serious, mature young lady and Eric remained the immature jokester. He's always been this silly, playful person that enjoys doing things I didn't think was funny. He knew how to get on my last nerves and make me smile at the same time, he still does to this day. We had our share of ups and downs like any other ordinary teenage relationship. Love, hate, breakup, get over it, makeup, only to repeat the same cycle over again and again. There were times when we tried, well, he tried dating other people, but something always led us back together. We became each other's "stronghold", but in a good way.

Eric was my first everything. Yes, literally my first. He was the first person I looked forward to seeing on the bus and at school each day, talking to on the phone after school, and his voice was the last thing I wanted to hear before closing my eyes at night. My heart thumped with excitement at the thought of seeing him on Wednesday nights and Sunday morning church services. He was like a magnet to me and I was attracted to everything about him: His smile, his laugh, his personality, and even his aggravating sense of humor. I loved his heart, humble nature, and his gifts and talents. We were both the musicians at our church; I was the piano player and he was the drummer. He also played the piano, but I loved hearing him play the drums more. Watching the way he'd nod his head to the beat, bite his bottom lip, and stick out his chin with every drum roll sent chills down my spine.

I can't say that I felt the same way about him playing the piano though, in my opinion, he's anointed to play the drums and playing the piano is more of a talent for him. We still go back and forth about who's the better piano player! Of course, I was the better technical player, but he was more creative on the keys than I was. I learned to play the piano by ear at a young age and ended up taking lessons to help me read music. Eric also played by ear and could read music a little, we both played the violin in middle and high school as well. The love of music is something we share and it knits us together.

The Promise

I was 15 years old when God spoke to me and showed me a vision of Eric as my husband. He gave me a feeling of purpose for our union, but didn't show me everything. I didn't share it with Eric or anyone else because I questioned whether or not I was just infatuated with him that much or if it was really God speaking. I mean, the dream of living happily ever after with my "Prince Eric" was nice and worth holding on to and adding a dog named max to the equation would only be icing on the cake! Then again, I was still young and had a lot more living to do and I didn't want to limit myself to him only. But, no matter how hard I tried to be or even see myself with someone else, all I could see in my future was him.

On my 16th birthday, Eric bought me an Oreo ice cream cake (my favorite) and presented me with a promise ring to solidify his "ownership" of me, as he called it. I never asked him for a ring, so it took me by surprise that he thought that much of me to even purchase one. My sister and I didn't have a sweet-sixteen birthday party, so on our 17th birthday our parents gifted us a huge party at our home. Oh! I forgot to mention, by this time we actually lived in a house, no more trailer treasure! My parents had it built directly behind our trailer and though it seemed like forever to build, I was so happy! Not having to worry about blowing away in those Florida hurricanes was such a relief and talk about the joys of having my own bedroom! Yes! I was totally there for it!

We invited all of our family and friends from school to the party. The word spread rather quickly and folks who weren't invited ended up showing up too. All was going well until some people from school who had a problem with a friend of mine crashed the party. An argument between them broke out in the street and I ran over to put a stop to it. I remember yelling and telling the uninvited person to leave. They were getting into their car and before I knew it, they were backing up in full speed headed directly towards me. I stood there paralyzed by the sight of their car quickly approaching me. Then out of nowhere, Eric came to my rescue and grabbed me before their car ran right into the car parked behind me.

I think I was more frustrated that they ruined our party more than I was shaken up about almost losing my life that night! Eric took me inside and tried to calm me down because I was heated, he then told me he didn't know what he would have done if he ever lost me. I immediately calmed down after hearing him say those words and it confirmed God's promise in my heart.

One Last Cry

Eric was preparing to graduate that May of 2002, we tried to spend as much time together as we could before he left for the army. After attending his Senior prom together, our relationship took a slight turn for the worst. Insecurities and uncertainty about our future contributed to discord between us amongst other things. There were people who didn't want us to be together, including the devil himself, but Eric was the one person in this world that I felt was worth fighting for.

The night before Eric left for basic training in the army he brought over a few of his possessions he wanted me to have, one of the items was a black stereo. Back then it was the norm to have stereos so we could record songs on the radio and listen to CD's we burned from the internet. He knew I didn't have one of my own, so giving me his was a kind gesture. I'd made a CD with some of our favorite slow jams and figured that night was the perfect opportunity to play it. I placed the CD inside the stereo and turned it to the song, One Last Cry, by Brian McKnight. We sat on the edge of the bed glaring into each other's eyes, then Eric stood up and reached for my hand. He pulled me close to him and began swaying back and forth, his embrace told me this was goodbye for us.

I wanted to hold onto him forever because I was afraid to let him go, I feared losing him to someone else. It's said that when you love someone you have to let them go and trust that what's meant to be will be. I wasn't ready to find out if there was truth to that statement. He grabbed me a little tighter, rested his head on my shoulder, then silently began crying. Somehow, I knew what he was saying without him having to speak a word. It was time for us to step into the unknown, for our relationship to be tested, and for us to see if we were truly meant to be together. As the song ended our lips softly brushed against each other's one last time.

We kept in touch and wrote letters while he was in basic training, though we were no longer a couple, I carried him in my spirit. He asked me to come to his basic training graduation and I wasn't sure if I could make it, but I wasn't going to say no without trying first. Luckily, he was like a son to my mother and she agreed to go. We made the 10 plus hour drive to South Carolina just to show our support and the whole ride there I felt butterflies in my stomach at the thought of seeing him. Though Eric and I didn't have a title, he still belonged to me in my heart. I knew what God had said and that settled it for me.

After the graduation, he came home for Christmas break before reporting to his first duty station in Fort Drum, NY. My mom knew he was coming and I remember her telling me with somewhat of a slight attitude, "don't be stupid." There are many scriptures in the bible that confirm warnings come before destruction. I knew exactly what my mom meant, she was warning me and although her intentions were good, her delivery made it hard for me to receive it.

The Guilt of My Mistake

Eric arrived home and the chemistry between us was undeniable. A solid relationship between us still wasn't in the picture, but because of our friendship, hanging out as exe's didn't really phase us. We spent time together and did things that made it seem like we were still a couple: Hugging, brushing each other's finger tips when walking together, trying to avoid holding hands, spending hours talking on the phone at night.

Things felt somewhat like normal again, I even went the extra mile to see him the day before he left for New York. I pretended to be sick one day and skipped school to go spend time with him. Then, after he left things went back to normal with my life as a senior in high school and he was off to new beginnings in New York. Almost two months went by and I was preparing to walk across the stage as an honor graduate from High school. I could have graduated early, but decided to finish out the year with my friends, I had already received my acceptance letter from the University of South Florida in Tampa where I would be starting my undergraduate studies in the Fall and things were lining up the way I'd imagined, at least that's what I thought.

Out of nowhere I started feeling fatigued and having cramps. Every day after school I would go home and jump straight in bed without doing homework or chores. I figured it was because my monthly cycle was about to begin but, it didn't. Then, I found out that I was pregnant! What on earth was I thinking that day? The ONE time we didn't use protection and POOF! PREGNANT! Really? I am not quite sure what I was thinking, but I wasn't prepared for what was to come. All I could remember was my mother warning me. By this time Eric was getting used to his life as a soldier and I was preparing to find my life outside of my parent's home. Do I tell him? How am I going to tell my parents? I dreaded telling him the news, but I feared for my life at the thought of telling my parents.

I made the dreadful call to Eric after confiding in a friend about my pregnancy. I remember feeling nervous and sick to my stomach as I waited for him to pick up the phone. "Hello," he said. Hesitantly, I whispered... "Eric, I'm pregnant." The phone went completely silent and I swear he stopped breathing for at least thirty seconds. I didn't know how he was going to respond, but I hoped he would reassure me that everything would be okay. I imagined his eyes were wide open and his jaw must have been touching the ground by now. I'm sure he was in just as much shock and disbelief as I was. The first thing he asked was if I was going to keep the baby, I didn't know if he was subliminally telling me to get an abortion or if he was really trying to see what my intentions were. I wanted to be angry with him for asking me such a thing, but I understood his reasons.

Life in the army was new to him and my dream of becoming a first-generation college graduate was important to me. As a teenager who was getting ready to take on the world with no clue of what to expect, I was scared. I don't make any excuses for my decision to have sex with Eric outside of marriage; it's a decision that we both made and a decision that we both live with to this day. As mentioned earlier in my book. I know that the Lord is sovereign and I believe that He still had a plan for me, as He does for you, as He does for us all. In this society and with most teenage pregnancies, you are told that you have many "options". Yet, even though I knew that I made a mistake, I didn't want to make an even bigger mistake by aborting our unborn child. Of course, because of fear I wrestled with the idea of having an abortion in my head, but I wasn't sure that I would have been able to live with the decision to sacrifice my unborn child just to selfishly live life on my own terms.

I knew my parents would be upset and others would be shocked by the news of my pregnancy. I could hear the voices in my head of what people would say: "Tacondra? Pregnant? No, not the smart, innocent one, she's the good girl! She's the last one we'd expect to get pregnant". They viewed me differently and some would even laugh at my demise, I was even more afraid of what my mom would think because she got pregnant with my brother at the age of 16. Seeing history repeat itself would only shatter her heart. I'm sure that the last thing she ever wanted was for her daughter to follow in her footsteps, but I was doing just that. I had no idea where I would get the courage from to tell my daddy that his baby girl made a mistake, but I couldn't keep it a secret for much longer.

I must have been close to eight weeks pregnant by then and I ended up telling my mom's two younger sisters before breaking the news to her. They laughed because they knew she was going to kill me, but they smiled at the thought of having a great niece or nephew on the way. I talked them into sticking around while I delivered the news to my mom, having their support was nice but I wanted their protection more than anything. I was sitting on my bed and my aunts each stood in a corner of the room like my bodyguards when my mom came and stood in the doorway. She leaned up against the door frame and literally stared into my soul, the look on her face told me that she knew what I was about to announce.

Terrified, I slowly uttered the words, "mama, I'm pregnant." The room went dead silent for what seemed like an eternity. I sat there and watched as the expression on her face dropped. She looked extremely disappointed, sad, and hurt. Thankfully, she didn't leap across the bed to try and kill me, but I'll never forget her words before walking away: "I'm not taking you to get an abortion either." Well, there was the answer to that question I had. Later that night, as I was sitting on the edge of my bed with my head held down, my dad entered the room and came and fell to his knees in front of me crying. My mom had apparently told him everything. Filled with guilt and shame, I broke down and started to cry with him, tears I had been holding back from the moment I found out I was pregnant up until that point began to overflow. I let it all out and I apologized for my error. My daddy embraced me and told me that everything was going to be okay. Something I desperately needed to hear, although, I struggled to believe things would be. I wish I could say that I felt somewhat relieved after my parents knew they were going to be grandparents in a few short months, but I wasn't. This was only the beginning of a long journey ahead.

Church Hurt

The news of me being pregnant spread like a wildfire throughout the community and our small church. There were rumors that I got pregnant on purpose to trap Eric, I could understand their view but it was far from the truth. Even though I believed God's promise concerning me and Eric, I didn't go out of my way to intentionally get pregnant just to make sure God delivered on His promise. It was an honest mistake and I had to live with the consequences.

If you've experienced an unwed pregnancy in your church you know the typical reaction, it's a mixture of disappointment, condemnation, and pity. There I was, young and still on breastmilk in my faith walk and now having to deal with everyone looking down on me. I knew enough about God from the lessons and teachings that I received but I still lacked a personal relationship with God. I received Christ in my heart at a young age and I enjoyed going to church, but in all honesty, the only reason I went to church was because my mom made me go. Of course, seeing Eric every time was an added bonus. But I wasn't matured spiritually and the level of faith I had was only an extension of the faith my mom, grandma's, and my auntie Sheryll had instilled in me.

Playing the piano was something I enjoyed doing in the church. When Eric left for the army, I was left holding down the fort with my younger cousins. I was sat down from my position because I was pregnant, but I didn't understand why. I asked my mom why things were that way and she explained how she too had to sit down from singing in the choir, repent before the church, and ask for forgiveness before she was restored to the choir after giving birth to my brother. As if I didn't already feel ashamed and embarrassed, the last thing I wanted to do was stand before the church to be judged!

I needed someone to show me where the "rule" was in the bible that states those who sinned must be sat down from using their gifts to glorify God. Was this biblical principle or religious tradition that I was being held accountable to? I knew the life growing inside of me was not a sin, although fornicating and getting pregnant out of wedlock was. Don't judge me, but my logic back then was that even Mary got pregnant as a teen and Joseph didn't kick her to the curb from being his wife! Although, he did try to. I'm very well aware that Mary was impregnated by the Holy Spirit, but I wanted a biblical explanation for my punishment. I can't recall if I ever received one back then, but I realize that religious "traditions" played a role in my discipline. Religion and tradition in the church, something I grew away from as I matured in faith and developed a personal relationship with God over the years. I understood the reasoning for sitting me down was to discipline me just as a child is disciplined by his parents out of their love for him.

"My child, don't make light of the Lord's discipline, and don't' give up when he corrects you. For the Lord disciplines those he loves."

- Hebrews 12:5-6

As a young adult, I didn't know how to deal with church hurt and being offended. I didn't know how to take my hurt to God, especially since playing the piano was my form of worship and my gift back to God. So, I sat silently in the church pews for eight long months without worshipping or giving God glory. I felt useless, ashamed of the baby I was carrying, and all alone having to take on the shame of "our" sin. Eric wasn't there and I always wondered if he would have been sat down as well, or if they would have treated him differently? A dark cloud of guilt, shame, and rejection eclipsed over me in this season. My relationship with God wasn't destroyed, but, undoubtedly it was damaged.

I remember a prophet came and ministered at the church one Sunday. He stood at the front calling others to come forward and prophesied over everyone. I listened and watched with my head held down as he called out things and spoke into their lives. I tried my best to avoid making eye contact with him, then it happened. He looked me right in the eye and said, "why do I see a dark cloud hovering over you?", he called me to the front. I must have been around five or six months pregnant at the time. Okay, pause for a moment, I need to know is it just me or does anyone else get nervous when prophets spot you out of the crowd? I was so not looking forward to him telling me about all my secrets and whatever visions or words God had given him regarding my life at the time. (Remember, I was young and naïve). He starred into my eyes then started speaking about how I wanted to be a nurse and I had all these dreams for my life. The waterworks went to flowing! How did he know? He went on to say other things I can't remember, but before I sat down he told me he saw God moving me up north along the east coast and that God was going to do amazing things in my life. The only person up the east coast at the time was Eric. After church, one of the ministers at the time officially introduced me to the prophet and told him that God used him to confirm some things. She told him that my "soon-to-be husband" was actually up north in New York. He looked at me like he didn't remember a word he'd prophesied, meanwhile I was looking confused because Eric and I weren't even on good terms, let alone thinking about marriage. God must have been telling both of them some things that I clearly could not see, but still hoped for. This was another confirmation of God's promise.

Moment of Reflection

Church hurt is inevitable, although it may not always be intentional. I realize that my church family's intention was not to hurt me, but to discipline me. I can accept punishment for my wrong doings, I have no problem with that. I just didn't understand or agree with the religious traditions. I believe that religion and tradition is why most people, especially young adults, shy away from attending church and they turn away from Christ instead of being pointed to Him. Religion (law) and tradition can easily misrepresent the nature of Christ and the reality of why He died on the cross. We must be careful not to negate what Christ did on the cross and the sacrifice God made for our sins. Correction and rebuke is justified, but it must be done in love and provided to the individual with an understanding of why so that the sting of correction doesn't harden their heart towards God.

It took me some time to heal from the hurt, but if Jesus was hurt by his own people, who are we to think that we are exempt from being hurt by the ones who love us? I've experienced my share of discipline and persecution in other churches as well and I'm certain there's more to come. As I grow in Christ, I expect offenses to come but, I've learned that I don't always have to take the offense. If and when the offenses arrive, because they will certainly come, be sure to take them straight to God.

The Wait

As I rested on the sonogram table waiting anxiously to find out what the sex of the baby was visions of a little boy jumping into a truck to go fishing with my dad came to my mind, I desired to have a son. Badly. I thought that having a little boy would mean easy clothes shopping, simple haircuts and my one-way ticket to becoming a sports mom millionaire! "It's a girl!" the ultrasound technician shouted after fighting forever with the baby just to capture the image. All I could think about was who is going to do her hair? Eric was excited and thrilled about having a daughter when I shared the news with him, he desired to have a little girl.

For months, I waited for him to want me, to want us to be a family. A little over six months into my pregnancy and after graduating from High school I was ready to fly to New York to see him. My parents were willing to purchase my ticket as a graduation gift. At first, Eric seemed excited about the idea of me coming to visit, he'd finally have the chance to see me wobbling around and to feel his daughter dancing inside of me. As I was finalizing the plans he changed his mind about me coming, he didn't give me an explanation or reason at all. I didn't question him, I simply said okay and left it alone. I started working in a daycare to save up money for the baby, I remember calling him in the same week that I would have been there with him. He was driving, being silent, and acting very awkward on the phone, then I heard a female's voice in the background. "Who is that?" I asked. It was an ex from high school he dated who'd been living in Chicago. Before I could catch myself, the words slipped out of my mouth, "I hope that bleep is going to help you pay child support when this baby is born!" Then I hung up the phone, bear in mind I needed a little more Jesus back then. Talk about feeling humiliated and angry all at once! I was the one carrying his child and he told me NO just to tell this chick YES! I was so hurt! I resented him and harbored bitterness for months to the point of distress. I didn't care about going to see him anymore and he wouldn't dare make a trip to Florida to see me.

There were moments throughout my pregnancy I genuinely enjoyed, but I wasn't always grateful for the experience. I remember taking pregnancy photos around my 8th month and I passed them out to a few of my friends in high school. On the back of the photos I wrote foolishly, "keep this photo safe, because it may be the only time you see me like this!" I even spoke the words to a few people without giving it any thought. In my mind, it was a joke, but I really didn't have plans of getting pregnant again anytime soon.

My relationship with Eric remained uncertain and I wasn't excited about the thought of being a single parent. Months went by and despite my efforts to get over the offenses, I refused to let them go. It was around September of 2003 when Eric found out he would be deploying to war in Iraq. His orders confirmed he would be leaving in November, at this point, I was over bad news. On top of everything else, I now had to mentally and emotionally prepare myself for him to be away from his daughter for an entire year and hope that he would survive the war and return home safely. *Could things get any worse!* As the time drew near for baby girl's arrival I struggled with wanting Eric to be present for her birth.

I'd pushed him so far away in my mind and heart that it didn't matter to me if he was there or not, I was still disappointed, hurt, and angry. Nine months of being pregnant and all he had were pictures of my journey. From my view, he didn't deserve a drop of joy after all the pain I endured. I secretly prayed that he wouldn't witness her entry into the world, a prayer that I later came to regret and wished I never uttered. It is said that a thought unspoken dies unborn. Proverbs 18:21 reads, "The tongue can bring death or life; those who love to talk will reap the consequences." (NLT) I knew nothing about the meaning of this before, but I certainly understand the power of your confession now. Be careful what you speak because you might literally end up having what you say!

My Loss

It was midnight, October 13th, 2003 and the contractions were strenuous. Baby Amiyah was ready to make her debut and Eric was on the road heading from New York to Florida. My mom and grandma Liz drove me to the hospital in the wee hours of the morning. Mama was driving as slow as a sloth and then we had to stop and get gas on top of that! *What happened to being prepared? Really! who forgets to put gas in the car?* By the time we arrived at the hospital, which took forever, I was craving the sensation of a huge needle piercing through the middle of my spine to give me some relief. I was afraid of getting an epidural, but those labor pains got stronger and my level of tolerance got lower. Unfortunately, the needle didn't show up as quickly as I desired but when it did, it hurt oh-so-good!

I was in labor for approximately 11 hours, I'll never forget the name of the nurse that cared for me most of that day. She did her best to ensure that I was as comfortable as possible. She'd come in the room periodically and perform checks on me to see how far along I had dilated and if the baby was ready to come. At one point, she mentioned feeling Amiyah's head crowning, but she felt something like a band blocking the entryway to the birth canal. Her evaluation concerned me however, the pressure I felt in my backside indicating that it was time to push heavily outweighed my worry about whatever she was feeling at the time. I was ready to push my baby out!

My mama, Cara, and grandma Liz were in the room coaching me through the breathing exercises, (which did not work), and encouraging me not to push until the doctor arrived. Cara looked as if she was having the time of her life watching me suffer, she caught me sneaking pushes in a few times when I thought no one was paying attention. Not to mention the constipated look on my face probably gave it away, I barely made it but the doctor eventually walked in and it was time to push! "Push! Okay, relax. Breathe... Now Push!" I've never pushed so hard before in my life! I pushed to the point where well, let's just say something else came out other than the baby. Hey, don't judge me! If you've ever birthed a child you'll understand.

Embarrassed and half way in tears, I asked the nurse, "did I just..." she quickly cut me off, "Nooo, you di..." and before she could even finish her sentence, Cara blurted out, "Yep!! you sure did!" She thought it was hilarious! I just wanted to be invisible at that point. I pushed with every ounce of strength in me, but something wasn't right and Amiyah couldn't break through. My mom told me that blood spewed out with every push and it was something she'd never seen before. The doctor finally performed an episiotomy, which supposedly helped create enough space for Amiyah's head to break through. When most babies are born they are covered in a waxy, cheese-like substance called vernix, which serves as a protective covering while in the womb. Amiyah was completely covered in my blood. A few moments longer in the canal and she would have suffocated in it.

I didn't get the chance to hold her and bond with her right away. The room grew still and silent for a moment, I looked into her eyes long enough for me to crack a smile on my face before the nurses took her away. Then the noise around me resumed. The doctor kept compressing my stomach to deliver the afterbirth to no avail. I couldn't see what was going on because a sheet was held up in front of me, but from the looks on their faces I could tell there was an issue. A heavy, uncontrollable outflow of blood was pouring from my body, I was hemorrhaging.

The doctor made every attempt to stop it, but nothing worked. She mentioned the possibility of performing a hysterectomy as a last resort. At 18 years old, the only thing I knew about a hysterectomy was that a woman could no longer have children. "No!" I yelled. Although, having another child was the last thing on my mind, I didn't want a hysterectomy. As they were wheeling me out of the room my grandma, in her sweet little voice said, "think positive Condra, everything is going to be okay." The worried look on her face convinced me to believe otherwise, but I was more encouraged by her faith in God. I took a deep breath and tried to focus on grandma's words. "Be positive…"

I remember lying on the table gazing into the ceiling illuminated with lights as the blood continuously poured out from my body. I was barely conscious and struggled to tell the nurses and doctors surrounding me about the pain I was feeling inside of me. The words I uttered were inaudible. I could hear voices around me whispering, sympathetically, "she's only 18…." I eventually felt the pressure from the pulling and tugging going on inside of my body. I knew they were doing the thing I dreaded the most. Hours later I opened my eyes to find myself in a room surrounded by family and friends. I was lethargic and immobile because of the blankets they wrapped me in firmly to regulate my body temperature and to control the swelling from all the fluids.

My mom came to my bedside holding Amiyah in her arms. I looked at her and asked, "Mama what happened to me?" Her voice cracked a little as she uttered the words, "you have your one…thank God for your one." With my head turned sideways I watched her walk away looking somewhat broken, but grateful to have her granddaughter in her arms. I looked around and saw other faces, many of which I could not make out because of being heavily sedated. I searched the room for his face and did not find it. Completely oblivious to the time, I just figured he was still on the road and would show up as soon as he could. A heavy tear left the corner of my eye and rolled slowly down my face before saturating my pillow. The silhouettes in the room started to fade again as I fell back into a deep sleep.

The next day I was told that the physician attempted everything possible to avoid performing the hysterectomy, but the anesthesia started to wear off and I'd lost too much blood to try anything else. Therefore, she was left with a decision to make: my life or my womb. The reality of what happened to me hadn't really set in. I was still digesting everything and all I really wanted to know was if Eric had arrived safely, I still hadn't heard from him. It was sometime in the afternoon when I called to find out where he was, he made it to town, but didn't come straight to the hospital. After the phone call, he said he would be on his way. I had mixed feelings about seeing him for the first time since that day I skipped school and wasn't sure how I would react, but I wanted him to see his baby girl. I wanted him to see that SHE was real. When he finally walked through the door a flood of emotions swarmed me.

I felt like crying, screaming, punching him in the face and kissing him all at once. I sat propped up in the hospital bed as he approached me with a solemn look in his eyes. Then he did the unthinkable, he leaned in to me and gave me a kiss on my lips. I wish I could have seen the look on my own face, I'm sure it wasn't pleasant. In what should have been a delightful, joyous moment for both of us the only thing I could think about was how Jesus felt when Judas betrayed him with a kiss. In other words, I felt like I had been kissed by the devil himself. Was it his way of apologizing for his stupid actions and decisions or was he merely feeling sorry because of what he heard happened to me?

I didn't even care to have that discussion with him. He was there and the look in his eyes when he held Amiyah for the first time was all that mattered. It was life changing for him to see that this little life he helped create was real. He'd seen pictures of me throughout the pregnancy and I sent him copies of the sonograms. Still, nothing made it more real than to hold his little girl in his hands. The following days in the hospital were extremely uncomfortable for me,

I couldn't nurture Amiyah the way I wanted to because the nurses and doctors spent so much time monitoring me.

I was given a blood transfusion during the surgery and received so much fluid that I no longer looked like myself. They drew my blood so many times, I felt like an addict with all the needle marks and blown up veins in my arms. To make matters worse, the doctors inserted and stitched up some kind of gauze or "packing" inside of me to stop the vaginal bleeding. When the time came to remove the stitches, I likened it to the feeling of a shoe string with sharp pieces of glass lined along the edges being unlaced through the holes of a shoe. I would have almost rather died on that operating table than to endure that painful aftermath.

After a few days in the hospital, it was finally time to go home. Eric loaded up his blue Mazda Protégé with our things and tucked Amiyah away safely into her car seat before helping me into the car. When I sat down the first thing I noticed was a pack of Newport cigarettes sitting on his dashboard. Keep in mind, I was oblivious to the new lifestyle he'd adapted to in the army. "Oh, so you smoke cigarettes now?" I asked him. He knew that I grew up with parents who smoked cigarettes and I couldn't stand the sight or smell of them. "Yeah…you want me to quit?" he asked nervously. In no way was I excited about his new habit, but who was I to tell him what he could and couldn't do? It really didn't matter as long as he didn't smoke around me or my child. When we arrived at my parent's house they were waiting eagerly to welcome home their first grand.

Eric spent the night to assist and to spend time with Amiyah. He was extremely helpful with taking care of her. Watching him patiently walk up and down the hall to soothe her late at night, hearing him talk to her, witnessing the way she looked in his eyes and smiled, and watching him fall asleep with her lying on his chest made every bit of pain I suffered worthwhile.

The second night he was there I gathered the nerve to ask him about "us'. It caught him off guard, but it was the elephant sitting in the room that needed to be addressed. I should have thought twice before I asked because I wasn't prepared for his response. He told me that he was in somewhat of a relationship with someone back in New York. The feelings I buried inside and refused to deal with for months immediately resurfaced. I began crying and yelling at him, "why are you here? Why would you come here and lay next to me, kiss on me, and pretend like we're all good if you have a girlfriend and no intentions of being with me?" This would have been the ideal moment for me to be dramatic and slap him, like they do in the soap operas, but I didn't. I never even considered that he might have been confused, vulnerable, and as emotionally unstable as I was.

Nonetheless, I felt disgust towards him, but I was too torn to do anything other than cry my heart out. He didn't know what to say or how to respond. He just sat there quietly. He looked at me and asked, "do you want me to leave?" I wish I could tell you that I was brave enough to tell him to get out of my face and bold enough to walk him out the door, but I didn't have the strength to push him away. "No…"

I whispered, before turning my back towards him and silently crying myself to sleep. Once again, I was hurt. This time I made up in my mind that I would let go any hopes of us being a family together. I would move on with my life and hope that someone else would want me, love me, and accept my child.

Eric spent the remainder of his time left taking Amiyah around to visit his family members and spending quality time with her. He took us to our one-week follow up appointment and Amiyah was healthy and doing well. The doctor didn't bother going into much detail about what happened to me the day I gave birth and I didn't care to talk much about it myself. She simply informed me that I would not be able to carry another child and would need a surrogate if I ever wanted more children. The reality of having a hysterectomy hadn't sunk in yet, and after all I'd gone through the thought of ever having another baby simply frightened me. I subconsciously accepted my fate. One thing the doctor failed to tell me about was the effect the hysterectomy would later have on my body. Having the surgery put me in a state of instant menopause. Two weeks flew by and before we knew it Eric was saying goodbye, again. This time, it was goodbye to his daughter. I was ready for him to leave, although I was sad about him heading off to war. The day he left I gave him a book of photographs to take with him, he kissed Amiyah goodbye and drove away.

Moving On

We remained in communication before he deployed to war in Iraq that November. Once he got over there we couldn't talk as often nor did we have the ability to video chat like we do nowadays. I used disposable cameras, voice recorders, and a camcorder just to keep him involved with her growth. I kept a photo of him in her crib so that she wouldn't forget his face and I recorded his voice so that she would recognize it. I sent him many pictures, voice recordings, videos, and care packages with some of his favorite snacks just to give him something to look forward to. I knew being away at war wasn't easy for him after having a newborn baby and regardless of our status, I knew it was important for us to maintain a friendship. After all, we had a child to raise together.

I started getting used to life without him. I enrolled into the local community college, started a new job, and was slightly interested in getting to know new people. By "people" I mean other men, but I wasn't ready to be in a relationship. Fast forward a few months and Eric was on his way home for R&R; a military term used for rest and recuperation. Amiyah was about six months old. I was happy about him seeing his daughter, but I was nervous about reconnecting with him after being at war. I didn't know what he had been exposed to over there or what to expect as far as his demeanor. His mom arranged a welcome home dinner for him at a restaurant in Plant City. The moment he laid eyes on Amiyah his face lit up with delight.

She didn't know who he was at first, but the more he talked to her and the longer she gazed into his eyes, the more relaxed she became in his arms. She remembered who he was. My heart flooded with emotion as I sat there watching him hold her. I began to feel all warm and fuzzy on the inside and it was only a matter of time before I saw the invisible hearts popping up over his head. Ugh, I couldn't believe he still had that effect on me.

We made the most of our time spent together as a "family" while he was there. Date nights, trips to theme parks, and enjoying late nights up taking photographs with Amiyah made the two weeks fly by way too fast. What was unusual about our time together was that not once did we talk about our status nor did we officially establish ourselves as being in a relationship. We kind of just went with the flow of things and took advantage of each other and the time we had. Of course, that means we did things we had no business doing. I wish I could remember the emotions I felt and the thoughts going through my mind during this time of bonding. I knew deep inside I still loved him, but I forced my heart to believe that he was no longer my desire.

When he left to go back to Iraq I felt indifferent about him, he was gone and I was back to doing life as I knew it. To this day, if you ask him what our relationship status was when he left to go back to Iraq he would say that we were a couple. I don't recall us having that conversation but, apparently, he thought that me giving him access to my body meant I belonged to him. I won't argue with that. While he still had access to my heart, a part of me still longed to experience something and someone new. Little did I know that I would run into that "someone" a few weeks later.

A Mystifying We

He focused his attention on me as I walked down the pavement with Amiyah wrapped up in my hands, looking for a place to sit in the stadium. He and his family were sitting toward the top. They were there supporting his brother, who performed in the high school track meet and I was there to support my family. The smile on his face brightened as I approached the area to sit nearby. It was the same smile I resisted falling for in his past attempts to get my attention. His presence alone made me feel a way I could hardly explain. I felt nervous, intimidated, intrigued and confused all at the same time. I wasn't sure if it was because he was older than me or because he was way more experienced in the relationship department than I was. Nevertheless, I couldn't deny that I was attracted to him, but I refused to let him know that.

Out of respect and for my own reasons, I choose not to disclose this individual's name, but he knows who he is and so does Eric. I don't remember exactly when we met, but it was through "mutual friends." I recall him having a thing for me when I was a junior in high school. We often ran into each other after football games or events that took place in the city. I didn't know much about him personally, or about his reputation but that probably had a lot to do with why he was attracted to me. Or it could have been that I was just another innocent female he was preying on? Who knows? I didn't know nor did I really care at the time. We ended up exchanging numbers that night and after our encounter I didn't see him again for a few weeks. In the meantime, I was looking for a daycare provider for Amiyah since I'd started a new job and my mom was preparing to go back to work as well. I was referred to an in-home-daycare provider in town and it just so happened that the owner was his mother.

I remember the day I went to speak with his mom about enrolling Amiyah into the daycare. I instantly fell in love with her beautiful spirit, kind heart, her wonderful sense of humor, and her smile that can light up an entire room. We were sitting next to each other having a conversation then suddenly, he walked through the door. I was a bit surprised to see him, although I didn't know why. I guess I wasn't expecting him to actually be there, he walked straight up to me, kneeled down beside me, looked me in the eyes, and said to his mother, "Mama, this is the one right here." Puzzled, I looked at him like, "What one?" Again, I was still hesitant about giving him my time or attention, but he was persistent and bold. I kind of liked it too! The way he stared into my soul as he declared those words took me by surprise and frightened me in an awkward yet, delightful way. Whether he meant it or not, I didn't know and it really didn't matter to me at the time. I quickly laughed at his comment before brushing it off and wrapping up my conversation with his mother in an attempt to escape, but he followed me out to my car.

I don't recall the exact dialogue between the two of us that day, but he didn't hold back his fondness of me. Before he could say anything else, I quickly cut him off and said, "you don't want me...I can't give you what you want in life" he looked confused. Here he is telling me how interested he is in me and all I could tell him in return was how I WASN'T what he wanted and what I COULDN'T give him in life! I had no idea about what he even wanted in life! But something inside of me knew he desired to have a rather nice size family one day.

To help him understand, I told him about my inability to physically birth children. Here we go again, of all the things I could have said or done to push him away why would I tell him this? And so soon! You would think that I would have at least let the man fall in love with me before informing him of my "secret" like they do on the Maury show! But no, instead my identity and worth became twisted up in my condition. My inadequacy became the measure by which I defined my worth and it told me what I could or could not have and who could or could not love me. This is when the lie that shouted that I was worthless, undeserving and that I could never be another man's desire manifested.

I must pause right here to ask the young single-parents, the divorcee who is left with more than one child to co-parent or raise on your own, to the person whose innocence has been violated, to the one who feels abandoned by their mother, father, or family members—what lies has the enemy deceived you into believing about your worth because of your loss? I want to cast down those lies now! The devil is a liar and there is no truth in him! Know that you are worthy of love, joy, peace, happiness, second chances, respect, and you absolutely deserve God's best!

I'll never forget his response that day. With a solemn look in his eyes he stated that maybe it wasn't meant for him to have kids and if so, we could adopt. He was sincere about it, however, I disregarded the nonsense coming from his mouth and told him how he needed to be with someone who could give him the family he wanted. Telling him I wasn't worthy didn't keep him from learning more about me though. I had no choice but to run into him more often after enrolling Amiyah into the daycare.

He was very much aware of my status with Eric, which was completely amicable at the time, although Eric was more interested in having a solid relationship with me. Being at war must have put some things into perspective for him, nevertheless my attention was elsewhere. I didn't allow myself to get too close to this other guy because he too had a girl that he'd supposedly been in and out of a relationship with. I understood what he was going through, considering the emotional roller coaster I was used to being on with Eric.

One day, I was picking up Amiyah and he asked me to accompany him to see about getting a stereo system installed in his car. I was hesitant at first, but didn't see any harm in going for a ride, so I agreed to go. As we were in route back to his house we passed his girlfriend at the time. When she saw his car she immediately turned around and came back towards the house. I didn't know what to expect, but I was certainly not in the mood for drama. From my viewpoint, I wasn't a threat to what they had going on although, I'm sure she didn't perceive it that way. He and I were just friends and I didn't want someone who was taken. Period.

I got out of the car said hello, and went inside while they stayed outside to talk. I was sitting in the living room when he finally came inside. Obviously, their conversation didn't go too well by his demeanor. He told me she asked who I was and his response was, "Ms. Wright." Why he used my last name at the time, instead of my first name, I still don't know, but it certainly didn't help the situation. He didn't mention much about what was said during their conversation but he implied that they were "done". I sat down on the chair in the living room feeling like somewhat of a stumbling block. He got down on his knees in front of me again, then out of the blue he leaned in and kissed me. "What was that about!" I asked surprisingly. He shrugged his shoulders. I didn't know how to feel and I didn't understand why he kissed me or if it meant anything, I don't even think he knew why he did it. Shortly thereafter, the dynamics of our relationship began to change.

The more time we spent talking on the phone and hanging out together I got to see a different side to him. We discovered things and interests we shared like making music, writing lyrics, and poetry. Our love for music was an automatic attraction for me and it didn't make it any better that he too was a drummer! Especially since I was already fascinated with Eric playing the drums. He was also prior military, something else he and Eric had in common. As time passed by, him and his family embraced Amiyah as if she was their own.

Often times, his mom would make little jokes about adopting and giving Amiyah their last name, but I believe she knew who really had my heart. I remember one day she helped me prepare a care package to send off to Eric, she taught me how to break down the goodie boxes so that I could add more stuff to the box. Clearly, she knew I had a thing for her son, but she must have known that I still loved Eric. I appreciated her understanding nature and unselfish stance.

Though Eric had my heart, this guy had my attention. I was captivated by him and only a few months had gone by. Literally, all of this happened within a five to six-month timeframe. We wrote a poem together that started with the words: "A little bit of you and a little bit of me would soon switch respective places into a mystifying we." It was a mystifying we, indeed. I wanted to give him my heart, but I couldn't. On one hand, it was because I felt inadequate and didn't believe he could ever love me, let alone consider me to be his wife one day. On the other, I was still holding on to the promise God made me concerning Eric.

I wrestled with my heart being torn between the two, I did my best to avoid making anything official with this individual. Anytime he would imply that we were in a relationship I'd respond with, "it's not that serious". I had no idea how much those words offended him, but I was afraid to love him. Or maybe I was afraid to have him love me back? I'm not sure, but after a few months we eventually grew apart. Me pushing him away didn't help and he didn't hesitate to move on. Seeing how easy it was for him to move forward pushed me right back into the arms of my comfort zone…Eric.

After not speaking or seeing the individual for a few months, we eventually crossed paths while driving through the neighborhood one day. When he saw me he immediately stopped his car in the middle of the street. So, I did too. I let down my window as he approached. I'll admit, it was nice seeing him again. We said hello and he asked how I was doing. I told him all was well and then he noticed a picture of me, Eric, and Amiyah sitting in the dashboard of my car. It was a photo we'd taken while he was home visiting that I kept tucked away in my purse. He pointed to the picture and said inquisitively, "oh yeah?" Alluding to the idea that Eric and I had reconciled our relationship. I looked him in the eyes, nodded my head and responded, "yeah." I can't really put into words the look I remember seeing on his face at the time, but he smiled somberly, wished me well, and returned to his car.

As I reflect on my involvement with this person, I must say that I am grateful for what it taught me, although I'm not proud about some of my actions. I walked away knowing that Amiyah could be loved by another family and that I could possibly be another man's desire. He was the only other "relationship" I'd experienced outside of Eric. For me, it was proof that I could be with someone else, maybe even him. Nevertheless, God's promise directed my heart and led me back to His will. His purpose. My Prince Eric.

Changed My Name

A few months after Amiyah's first birthday Eric returned from overseas. A few months later I received a card from him in the mail. Inside the card was a card, a beautiful, marquise-cut, diamond ring, and a written message that said, "Will you marry me?" Honestly, I was a bit thrown off by the proposal. I mean, I didn't have a dream proposal back then anyway, but I never imagined it would be by mail! Don't laugh, but I still thought it was the sweetest gesture! I'm not really a hard person to please. Well, at least I wasn't back then. I enjoy giving and receiving gifts, so the thought was what counted to me. I'm still not sure what he was thinking sending me an expensive engagement ring in a card through the mail! But he did and guess what fool couldn't resist saying no? Yep-this girl!

As much as I couldn't stand him, I loved him and I knew in my heart and spirit that God's promise would come through. We couldn't afford to have the dream wedding I never imagined. I was broke, he was broke, and both our parents were broke too! It didn't matter though. Eric wanted to have me and Amiyah with him in New York. Instead of taking our time to actually plan a wedding, he flew me out to New York to marry him.

Though it was delayed for quite some time, the promise God made me was not denied! I would finally make my presence known in Watertown, New York and I was heading there for Eric to change my last name! On March 26th, 2005, we had a small ceremony at the local church he attended there. I still regret stripping our family and friends of witnessing our special occasion. Furthermore, my dad didn't have the opportunity to walk his baby girl down the aisle. However, we promised that one day we would have our dream wedding in Florida for all to see and so my father could properly give me away.

That Saturday, the members of the church were just finishing up choir rehearsal before our ceremony began. We didn't have anyone to invite, besides a few of Eric's army buddies, so we welcomed whoever was present and wanted to stay to be our guests. I wore a simple but classy, long, satin, ivory-colored gown that accentuated whatever curves I had at the time, and a satin shawl was wrapped around my shoulders. I slid my hair over to the side and tucked a fresh flower from the bouquet Eric had made for me behind my ear. Eric wore his army dress blues, which is what the men wear to a military ball. His best friend at the time stood beside him as his best man. Unfortunately, I didn't have my best friend there but, thankfully, one of the women at the church stood in her place.

I entered the church walking down the aisle to the song "Forever" by Dave Hollister. I remember feeling nervous and shaky, I could have definitely used my daddy's arm to lean on as unclear images of my future flashed before my eyes. The closer I got to Eric the more focused I became in his eyes. I didn't know what to do at the moment, except feel the butterflies in my stomach and avoid passing out. He reached for my hand and smiled in an effort to calm me down. I could tell he was nervous too. Then he looked me in the eyes and whispered a joke to me. I wish I could remember what he said, but it made the both of us laugh and it helped ease the jitters. While standing at the altar the priest presiding over the ceremony asked, "who here gives this bride away?" I looked around a bit confused because I was certain that my father wasn't there and then out of nowhere I heard my daddy's voice say, "I do." "Say it a little bit louder", the woman said as she held a microphone up to the cell phone. "I do!" he yelled again. WATERWORKS! I cried because back then we didn't have facetime or anything of that nature so just to hear his voice and the kind gesture of making sure my dad was able to do his part in our ceremony made my day.

After saying our vows and I do's, Eric became my king and I finally became his queen. We then rode off into the sunlight in his vibrant blue Mazda Protégé and headed to our lavish honeymoon at the Syracuse Mall! Hey, remember we were young and broke, so don't judge us! After enjoying dinner at a restaurant that overlooked the food court we headed to an area where people were having fun ice-skating, then he took me back to the hotel for the night. I jumped in the shower to prepare for our first night as a married couple! Praise Jesus! He snuck away and went to a local grocery store while I was freshening up. By the time I was done there was a small wedding cake on the table with a sweet-scented candle lit beside it. We cut our first slice of cake together and relished in our love for each other the rest of the night. I was excited and nervous about this new chapter in our lives.

Pregnant at the age of 17, a mother at 18, and now a wife at 19! Life was happening way too fast and little did I know that taking on a whole new identity as an army wife wouldn't be easy. I went back to Florida and worked for a few months before making the big move. Finally, Eric came to take us away with him. It was hard for me to leave my parents after they'd helped me so much with Amiyah for the past year and a half. It was even more difficult for them to let go of their first grandbaby. Away we went and my focus became solely on being a supportive wife to my husband and a mother to our daughter. I had to learn a lot on my own and finding the balance between being a military wife, a mother, and trying to figure out who I was as an individual became a struggle. I placed my passions, dreams, and desires for myself on the back burner and focused my efforts on supporting and helping my husband advance his army career. The more I discovered my new identity in him, the less I remembered about my own self.

The Reality of Marriage

The first year of marriage flew by. Eric and I later moved back down south to Texas, thank God. I'd had enough of the cold weather and lack of vibrant colors in upstate New York. I vividly remember on the day we got married a woman approached me in the church after the ceremony. She told me to lift my hands, so I did. She then took the palm of her hands and slapped them against mine and declared, "you do not have to fight!" I knew exactly what she was referring to. I inherited the instinct to fight after seeing my parents do it. The last thing I ever wanted to do was get into a brawl with my husband, but I knew very well the adeptness to fight was in me.

The first time became the last time we ever had a physical altercation. We had only been married for about a year, if that. I can laugh about it now because it was over something minimal and stupid, but all it took was for him to approach me the wrong way with a certain look in his eye. This was a distinctive look, I remember my father had that same look in his eyes when he and my mother were about to get into a brawl. Although our fight was nothing like theirs was back then, the little one-minute fight did occur and neither of us were proud of our actions towards each other. We made a decision to never put our hands on each other in that way again. Now, that doesn't mean we never had disagreements or arguments thereafter. We did and still do sometimes, but we've learned how to fight the true enemy together versus fighting each other. Disagreements are inevitable in marriage or any relationship for that matter, but inflicting pain on the person you love is a choice.

As I think about it, most of our disagreements were rooted in my pain. I used my loss as fuel to ignite or reignite the unwanted flames between us. The pain and reality of my loss reared its ugly head often in our marriage and ultimately took control.

My Loss, My Gain

I lost my identity when a part of me was taken. A part of me that made me who I was, made me who I am, and inspires me to become the woman I'm called to be.

I've been damaged- my mind and body almost to the point of no return. I hurt as the years go by. I drown in my tears as the memories come and go and the thoughts of "what life could have been like" seep through my mind.

A slow death inside of me transpired the moment it was seized from me; even while holding the life that it gave me in my hands. How could the one thing I lost be the very thing that kept me from my death?

I walk around each day with a smile on my face, when I really want to stare angrily at other women. I keep giving of myself, although, I'm empty on the inside. I portray happiness, when pain and sorrow are my two best friends.

I'm merely existing because living is beyond my reach. I cope with my loss the best I know how. Nevertheless, I am still vulnerable, embarrassed, and made uneasy by it. How am I supposed to endure life being bare? Not having the essence of what makes me a woman?

I lost a lifetime of precious moments to gain something so precious full of memories to share. I lost an unknown future to secure a future I now know by name. I lost a gift to be able to share a gift with others. A deep wound replaced my womb. Through my pain and suffering a tremendous gift was birthed.

My loss constantly attempts to overshadow my gain, but it will not rein; for I shall overcome it. But for now, the pain still owns me...

Owned By Pain

My mind and body deceived me into believing I could still get pregnant after having a total hysterectomy. The signs appeared every month around the time my menstrual cycle would come on, except I no longer bled. I took a bunch of pregnancy tests hoping to see positive results and sometimes I would feel random flutters in my stomach. The sensations were electrifying and reminded me of the moments I took for granted during my pregnancy. I almost felt normal again after feeling each sensation, but the scar that stretched from one side of my lower abdomen to the other constantly reminded me of my barrenness. It also reminded me of the bitterness that occupied a space in my heart toward my husband. For the first few years of our marriage I wouldn't let him touch or wrap his arms around my stomach.

The harsh reality that I could never carry another child for him, especially a son, hurt me to my core. He would never experience the joy of me being pregnant or ever witness the miracle of childbirth; at least not with me. Going out in public places or with groups of people was disheartening. People would see our family and ask, "Is she the only child? You guys don't want more?" From their viewpoint, we were a young couple with a promising future full of babies, toddlers, and more babies! They weren't aware of my condition or the circumstances surrounding it. Most people still aren't or they forget because in their eyes I'm still "young." The countenance on my face would fall every time someone asked me about having more children. Sometimes I wished that I was invisible or better yet I just simply ignored the question. Sometimes I responded with, "I'm happy with my one," a response I had rehearsed more times than I could count. Eric would quickly think of a silly comeback like, "Nope, one and done! We're good!" Or he would change the subject in efforts to shield me from shame.

Many nights I cried because of my inadequacy. I cried because I wanted another baby and couldn't have one. I cried because my daughter was lonely and wanted someone to grow up with and I couldn't give it to her. I even cried because other women around me could get pregnant and could share the experience with their spouses. Then there were other women who could still have children, although they didn't really deserve them. Many times, I questioned God, "Why me? What did I do to deserve this?" Was I being punished for writing foolishly on the back of those photos? Was it for the selfish prayer I uttered? And was Eric stuck with me paying the price?

Sipping on Poison

No matter how many times I tried to extinguish the fire burning inside of me to understand why and what happened to me that day, it wouldn't die down. I wanted quick answers to questions that I never knew to ask before. I remember seeking legal advice about a year after the incident occurred, but after investigating my case I was informed that I couldn't move forward with a pursuit because a pathology report revealed I was diagnosed with Acute Chorioamnionitis-A bacterial infection that occurs before or during labor and can lead to serious complications including: bacteremia (infection in the bloodstream), endometritis (infection in the lining of the uterus), the need for a cesarean delivery, and heavy blood loss with delivery and blood clots.

The most common risk factors for this condition includes "maternal age less than 21 years old, first pregnancy, long labor, multiple vaginal examinations during labor, ruptured membranes (the water has broken) for an extended period, and excessive fetal or uterine monitoring." I matched a few risk factors, but not all of them. I was told that with this condition I had no choice but to give birth normally to prevent further complications or the death of my baby. But something didn't make sense to me. I remember the nurse saying she felt a band-like object blocking Amiyah's head from entering my cervix, which I later came to believe was the placenta sitting low in my uterus. Placenta Previa is a condition where the placenta lies low in the uterus and completely or partially blocks the cervix. Pregnant women diagnosed with this condition MUST have a delivery by Cesarean-section. At the time I was young and uninformed, I went against my instincts in further pursuing the matter and settled with my fate, I kept telling myself to just be thankful that I was alive.

Fast forward a year or two and I decided to request my medical records from the doctor's office and hospital. I stumbled across a document that ripped my soul from my body. I was standing in the kitchen when I found a signed and dated consent form by me acknowledging that I would be given a C-section approximately three months prior to me giving birth. I pushed Amiyah out the day I gave birth to her, but apparently this form the doctors had given me stated that I needed to have a C-section. With all that was going on while I was pregnant, I honestly don't even remember signing the form or having a discussion about it. But it was in my records, just as clear as day.

I nearly choked due to the lack of air in the room. I struggled to breath as visions of a son, a daughter, twins, precious moments, and stolen memories I would never witness raced through my mind. I screamed out in despair as my body sank to the floor. I curled up into the fetal position and comforted myself with my own embrace, while I drowned in my tears. Eric was deployed again by this time and I was all the way in Georgia with no one to console me. That day, I consumed the last drop of poison from the pain I'd been sipping on.

Things only got worse from that point. Life with menopause made me forget I was in my 20's. Hot flashes, sweats, irritability, mood swings, hormonal acne, and unexplainable weight gain became my new best friends on top of the depression. The pounds of shame, guilt and low-self-esteem parked themselves right in the middle of my waistline, under my chin, and on my face, it was everywhere! The weight refused to go away regardless of how much I exercised or the amount of rabbit food I ate. I became hopeless and resorted to emotional eating at best to relieve the negative emotions. I didn't know how to be content with myself and being content with my marriage all at the same time was nearly impossible. I made Eric feel like he was failing as a husband because he couldn't fix me or love me the way I wanted to be loved. I honestly didn't know what I wanted! My pain produced fruits of overbearingness, ungratefulness, unhappiness, selfishness, and it birthed a sense of entitlement in me.

According to Webster's dictionary, the definition of entitlement is "the belief that one is inherently deserving of privileges or special treatment." The way I viewed it, I was entitled to special treatment and more considering all that was taken away from me. I had a right to be selfish. Since I was unable to take my frustrations out on anyone else, I automatically blamed my husband and God. Misplaced blame blocked me from giving Eric the respect and honor that he deserved. I understood that he was the head of our household, but my flesh would not yield to his authority no matter how hard I tried. I didn't know how to be the weaker vessel because being strong was all I knew how to do even if it meant faking it. The enemy would whisper lies in my ear like, "he can't handle a woman like you" or "he's too weak." *A woman like me? Yeah, A broken and damaged woman.* I needed someone to put my broken pieces back together. I wanted Eric to do it, but he couldn't, I was looking for "a man" to do something that only God could do.

The enemy made me question why Eric chose to marry me when he could have easily had someone else. I didn't understand how he could love me during a time when I struggled to love myself. By no means is Eric perfect, but he tried the best he could to love the hell out of me during this phase of my life. We are both flawed human beings, but he was a little more "whole" than I was during this time and I resented him for that.

We both contributed to our share of problems in our marriage, but I certainly didn't make it any easier for him to be happily married to me sometimes. One of my now favorite scriptures in Proverbs says, "A wise woman builds her house, but the foolish woman tears it down with her own hands" (14:1). Some mornings Eric would wake up to a wise, lovely woman, determined to build up our home and later he would return home to the foolish woman that was trying to tear it down.

He often looked at me and smiled with a heavy heart and in return I looked him in the eye, cut him deep with my eyes, and walk away without acknowledging his gesture. I was bitter and full of resentment, the lies I believed about myself and him negatively influenced my capacity to love him. I always felt as though my love for him was stronger than his love for me, especially when we were younger. But the tables were turned and I refused to believe that his love for me grew deeper simply out of remorse or pity for me.

The last thing I needed was for him to feel sorry for me, so I started telling myself things like, "he doesn't love you" or "you deserve better". Truth be told, I didn't deserve him. He wasn't the one resentful, bitter, or angry, he was free and I was bound. Bound to my misery and to the person I ultimately blamed with no justifiable reason. The saying is true that hurt people hurt people, my wounds bled out profusely and no matter how much I tried or he tried to make them stop they wouldn't. Spiritually, I was bleeding out all over again the same way I suffered in the natural years prior.

Dealing With Insecurities

I wanted Eric to feel my pain, although I knew he would never fully understand the weight of my burden. He still possessed every part of him that made him whole as a man. In the back of my mind, I knew he could easily step outside of our marriage and get another woman pregnant. I felt threatened by the thought. I remember we talked about him getting a vasectomy since I could no longer get pregnant. He was willing to do anything to please me, but my damaged thought process refused to let me make it easy for him to be unfaithful. I tried to use the stench of my infected wounds to push him away from me. I was really crying out for help, but didn't know how to tell him. The more I pushed him away, the less I could blame him for emotionally attaching himself to women who made him feel wanted.

My personal issues and insecurities spilled all over into our marriage, there was never a doubt in my mind that he loved me, but my attitude towards him became more repelling than it was attractive. I eventually started noticing small changes in his behavior: Sneaking away to make phone calls or send texts, using social media more often, changing passwords to his accounts, the things we typically do in relationships when we're attempting to hide something from the other person. It wasn't until God showed me the woman's face in a dream that confirmed what I had been discerning. He was emotionally attached to someone else.

We all have spiritual demons assigned to us. Are you aware of yours? I knew mine by name. Whether you're battling with a spirit of pornography, lust, adultery, idolatry, depression, rejection, reckless spending, or pride, we all have giants to defeat. I gave myself over to pornography and masturbation just to avoid consummating with my husband because I struggled with feeling wanted and I was ashamed of my widening body. My gift of discernment prevented a lot of situations in our marriage from turning for the worse over the years, but I began using my gift in the wrong way and for my own good instead of taking my discernments to God in prayer.

If you go looking for dirt on your spouse, trust me, you will find it. Whatever ounce of trust I had in my husband about him being faithful to me became obsolete. The emotional attachments he had with these other women hurt just as much had he slept with them. I always trusted that he would provide for our family, but I didn't trust him to lead, cover, or love me. For years, I placed Eric on a pedestal; I'm talking about since we were young! I made him an idol in my life and the moment I couldn't trust him to be faithful to me, my trust and faith in God became tainted. I'm very cognizant of how my behavior, attitude, and mindset contributed to my husband yielding to his demons and me to mine. There were many times I wanted to quit my marriage and walk away but, he would never accept getting the "D" word. Of all the things, jobs and people I left before, Eric was the one person my heart didn't know how to walk out on. For some reason, I just couldn't "quit" on him.

Defeat Over Victory

As the years went by I grew accustomed to living life in constant defeat, rather than endless victory. After being stripped of my joy, contentment, and self-worth, giving up became easy. Cultivating the gifts and talents God gave me became pointless and I lost all expectations of anything good ever happening to me. Worry and anxiety mastered my mind, no one ever knew that I was the person next door living with high-functioning anxiety.

Enjoying moments as they were, planning for the future, and exploring new ideas and opportunities was nearly impossible. The worst possible outcome in every situation was inevitable in my mind. Fear of the unknown deprived me of contentment. Do you know what it feels like to hand yourself over to worry and anxiety? I traced the root of my anxiety back to the day I gave birth my daughter. I remembered the doctor mentioning the possibility of having a hysterectomy. I also remember my grandmother telling me to "think positive". Thinking positively was something I tried doing that day, but despite my efforts, the thing I dreaded the most happened. This is when my core belief that positive thinking won't prevent negative outcomes was formed.

In my heart, I knew it was wrong to think that way but in my mind, it was my reality. My reality made it difficult for me to imagine, dream and even trust people. I closed myself off from others to protect my heart and I didn't allow myself to get to attached to people because I feared that they would figure me out. I was afraid that someone would see beyond the mask that I was wearing to disguise my agony. I never wanted anyone's pity, I simply wanted to feel whole and free.

Behind The Mask

If only you could see the real me, I wonder how you would feel. If you knew that I struggled with shame and disappointments, would you still look up to me?

If you knew that I was truly hurting inside would you still believe my smile? If I told you about my lack of feeling or emotions, would you think I was crazy for a while?

If I shared my most deep and darkest secrets with you, would you forever be in denial? If I told you that I was once the offender would you still care to emulate my lifestyle?

If I told you about the demons of my past that I still battle in war each day, would you have the courage to jump in and fight with me or would you turn and walk away?

If I told you I often felt hopeless and didn't believe that life was worthwhile, would you still receive an encouraging word from me in moments when you're feeling defiled?

If only you could lift the mask from my face that I so helplessly hide behind, surely, you would be surprised and perplexed by the disturbing truths you would find.

Behind the mask lives a stranger, one I'm afraid of getting to know. Beyond the mask rests a lifeless seed that hungers and thirsts for growth. Behind the mask lies a dreamer whose heart longs to see its dreams come true. Behind the mask lie gifts and talents that no one ever knew.

Behind the mask lie passions that have never been disclosed. Behind this mask lies purpose, and a life to live that has yet been chosen. Behind this mask lies a slave to fear one who is eager to be set free. Behind this mask, I'm a woman being held hostage and the adversary is...me.

Behind The Mask

I found comfort in wearing masks to conceal my pain. I walked around smiling on the outside for everyone else to see, but no one could hear me screaming on the inside. I was deeply broken. I felt worthless and forsaken by God, waking up each day seemed like more of a curse than it did a blessing. I disguised my pain with confidence, happiness, faith, and the appearance of wholeness just to get by. These masks offended the truth about who I was, yet satisfied the image of who people believed me to be.

At the age of 24 I finally broke the silence about my despair to my primary care physician. She diagnosed me with dysthymia depression and asked if I was interested in taking medication for treatment, I refused. I didn't believe in taking medication any more than I cared to lay on someone's sofa to talk about my misfortune. I kept telling myself that no one would understand what I went through; unless, they too had experienced it themselves. I named stinking thinking my therapist and prescribed isolation as my treatment. I built walls porous enough for others to access parts of me, but I confined my heart within parameters to protect myself from any more pain. Pain imprisoned me, took away my voice and made me a complete stranger to myself. It's said that an idle mind is the devil's playground, well I know this to be true for sure.

The enemy filled my head with more lies and deceived me into thinking that I was damaged goods; no longer fit for use or valuable. I attended church services praying for God to have mercy on me. I prayed for a miracle to occur that my faith didn't even have the capacity to receive.

I remember attending a 'Leaders That Lead' conference in Austin, TX with our church at the time and the Spirit of God fell heavy in the service. Our beloved Bishop prayed and prophesied healing over the entire congregation and then he prophesied that someone in the audience had something taken outside of their body by doctors. I stood there with tears falling down my face and my hand resting on my abdomen. He declared that God was going to restore what was taken. After the service, a friend of mine approached me and immediately stood in agreement that the prophecy was for me.

A part of me believed that God could perform this miracle if He so desired. On the other hand, I knew that it was naturally impossible. I mean, I heard of artificial wombs being created to clone animals and such, but I've never seen or heard of a woman without a womb physically carrying and birthing a child again. Possibilities in the spiritual were endless however, I was so discouraged by what I knew in the natural that believing in God's supernatural was impossible for me!

A few years later, I was sitting at home in a recliner one day crying and dwelling on this prophesy when suddenly I felt a leap in my belly. It startled me because it felt like a baby kicked me! God then spoke to my spirit and said, "You may not physically birth another child, but spiritually, you'll give birth to many." Words I'll never forget, although I didn't quite understand what He meant by it at the time. I was still battling with being carnal minded versus spiritual minded during this time, so I couldn't receive what God was saying to me in the Spirit.

Do you have a condition in the natural that the enemy is using to blind you to what God is doing or saying to you in the Spirit? You are in the middle of spiritual warfare and may not know it. The enemy was fighting to hold my mind captive so that he could do whatever he wanted with me. Although the spirit is willing, the flesh is weak. I was willing to hear God speaking to me, but I was too angry, bitter, and full of resentment in my flesh to receive it. I wanted another baby, I longed to relive the experience I once took for granted. I desired it not just for myself, but for Eric and Amiyah as well. I didn't share my personal battles with family or friends, not even my twin sister or mother knew. I confided in my best friend about marital issues from time to time, but nothing about the unseen battle in my mind.

I thought I was doing myself a favor by internalizing my pain. But some days I couldn't stand the pressure of holding it all in. I didn't want to live and I knew a spirit of depression was on assignment to take me out, especially since the devil failed to do so on October 13th, 2003. I entertained suicidal thoughts on multiple occasions. Most of the times were when Eric was deployed and Amiyah was too young to even know what I was doing. There were nights when I went into the bathroom and stood in front of the mirror, crying, holding a bottle of pills in my hand or a razorblade to my wrist. I prayed and cried out to God asking Him to give me a sign that showed me that my life was indeed worth living. I remember sitting inside a closed garage with the car running as I waited for the fumes to choke the life out of me. God's angels were surely watching over me because no matter what I did He always intervened. Amiyah would come knocking on the door calling and looking for me at just the right moment or the Holy Spirit would whisper softly in my ear "Stop. Put it down. Don't do that. I love you too much."

God would remind me that my daughter and husband were my reasons why I couldn't take myself out, and he always reassured me that everything that I experienced was for a purpose. There was purpose in my pain all along, but I couldn't see it. I was married to the man God promised me and together we shared a precious gift. But why wasn't it enough? Why was I depriving Amiyah of the mother she deserved and my husband of the wife he needed? We often starve to death the people who really matter the most, while we feed the lies, plots, ploys, and plans of the enemy. I was letting the devil get fat off of my pain and rob me of the life remaining inside of me.

Perhaps, you've walked through a valley like this before. You may be passing through a dark night of the soul in the season you're currently in. A season where the foulness of your pain continuously overshadows the beauty in your life. I want to remind you that this too shall pass. Some storms come to wipe you out, others come to reveal your strength. The one thing about all storms is that they don't come to stay, they come to pass! Therefore, if you're in a stormy season right now and you still have breath in your lungs and a heart that beats to a rhythm of its own, then know that God is not through with you yet! I know it sounds cliché but, believe me when I tell you it's the truth! If your purpose on earth was complete then it's safe to suggest that you wouldn't be reading this book right now. Furthermore, you wouldn't feel the need to play God by taking matters of your life into your own hands. If God wanted to, He could easily pluck you from this earth before your next eye blink.

I think about Jesus Christ's walk and work during his thirty-three years on earth. Remembering that Jesus was God in the flesh and could have easily removed himself from earth if He wanted to. In a much less painful way, might I add. But he didn't. In Matthew 26: 36-56 the bible talks about Jesus being at the garden of Gethsemane and how sorrowful and troubled He was. He fell to His face and prayed, "Father, if you're willing, take this cup from me; yet not my will, but yours be done." In the middle of His anguish, Jesus prayed earnestly for God to remove the death sentence from Him. His flesh wanted to live for it was weak but in His spirit, He knew this had to happen in order for the prophecies to be fulfilled. Jesus denied His flesh and relinquished His will to live for the Father's will instead. He became sin, the very thing God detests, so that you and I could have eternal life. He understood that His death would serve a purpose far greater than the pain, affliction, and crucifixion His body suffered. That is so powerful. Who can fully understand the power of Christ's death and resurrection? Many of us get so consumed with our brokenness that we forget Christ became fragmented so that we could be whole. So let me ask, do you believe you were worth His sacrifice?

Truth be told, I didn't always believe in my heart that I was worth His sacrifice. I struggled believing what the Word of God said about me because I didn't know what it said or where to find it in scriptures for that matter.

Why is it so easy for us to quote the two verses of scriptures we do know to help encourage others when deep inside we silently struggle to believe God's word for ourselves? I don't know about you, but I've definitely been the "doubting Thomas" disciple who walked with God, yet was still considered an "unbelieving believer." Such an oxymoron! We claim to believe God, but don't believe in what the Word of God says. The scripture 1 John 1:1 says, "In the beginning was the Word and the Word was with God, and the Word was God" (King James Version). You struggle to believe in the Word of God because of a lack of faith in the GOD of the word. Instead of asking, "Can God?" your confession and belief should be, "God Can!" Stop limiting God in your life! The value of knowing Christ is priceless. Once we truly come to grips with our Heavenly Father's loving, caring, sharing nature and character, trusting and believing in Him becomes easier. He is faithful in all things, He is a Redeemer, a Restorer, He cares for us and He watches over His word to perform it. The beauty is that God doesn't require us to understand all that He is doing, He only wants us to believe that He is who He says He is.

Love, God makes no mistakes. **Your presence on earth is not by error, no more than your departure from earth will be.** You can self-destruct and let the enemy deceive you into thinking your life is worthless, useless, and without purpose or you can focus on the truth of God's Word and allow it to transform your mind. You can live the abundant life, a life that glorifies God and edifies others because, remember, it's not about you! Someone out there, somewhere needs you to survive because their healing is dependent upon your obedience!

Rebirth

Nine years after giving birth I received the wonderful news that my twin sister would give birth to a baby girl. I was ecstatic about the chance to witness my niece enter into this world. The moment I found out Cara was pregnant I sensed the need to protect her. I feared that the same thing would happen to her as it did me. Protecting her would be a difficult task since she lived in Florida and I was living in Texas at the time. I wanted her to have a stress-free pregnancy and a healthy baby in the end. Unfortunately, her circumstances didn't allow her to live completely stress free. I knew that making the move wasn't easy for her, but I talked her into moving to Texas towards the end of her pregnancy. I'm so glad she agreed.

The memories of me being pregnant and seeing my sister's growing belly left me feeling nostalgic. I longed to feel and see a baby growing inside of me. I yearned for the pregnancy cravings, eating all the food I could without feeling guilty, and even the joys of putting up with late-night bladder works. Okay, maybe not the bladder works, but the rest of it, yes. I enjoyed every moment I witnessed of her being pregnant. September 17, 2012 finally arrived. I stood by my sister's side from beginning to end. Well, technically I didn't stand by her as they administered the epidural. I tried, but I nearly fainted at the sight of it!

The nurse ended up tending to me on the floor while I starred up at Cara hunched over on the edge of the bed getting a needle shoved into her spine. "You're supposed to be in here supporting me and here you have the nurses tending to you!" she yelled. The only thing I could do at the time was laugh. I wasn't sure if I was prepared for her to push the baby out just yet, but my hesitations certainly didn't stop the baby from coming. With each push, I became even more breathless as fear grasped me and the painful memories played over like a movie trailer in my head. Yet, I marveled at the miracle taking place before my eyes as the crown of Laila's head surfaced and she slipped her way right into this world. I let go a huge sigh of relief and cleansing waters fell from my eyes. Everything about the experience was breathtakingly beautiful and I even had the honor of cutting the umbilical cord.

I walked outside of the room to gather myself and the emotions overflowed. Many thoughts ran through my mind as I reflected on the aftermath of my own delivery. It may sound crazy, but I felt as though witnessing my sister's miracle allowed me to relive my situation, but with a positive outcome. I couldn't thank God enough for protecting my sister from having complications and for a healthy baby girl. Even though Eric didn't get to actually witness the birth, he did sit outside in the waiting room the entire time. As I walked through the double doors I tried to hide the tears falling down my face so that he wouldn't see how overwhelmed I was. He comforted me before going back into the room to meet the new addition to the family. Watching Eric as he held Laila and gazed into her eyes with the same sparkle in his own brought back beautiful memories of him holding Amiyah for the first time. Just him being there at the hospital waiting for Laila's arrival meant so much to me. It was as if somehow, he redeemed himself for not being there the day I gave birth to our daughter. From that moment almost nine years later, pieces of resentment slowly started chipping away from my heart and I knew this rebirth was the beginning of my healing process.

The Path to Recovery

There are layers to healing. It is a process that takes time, requires the Help of the Holy Spirit, and nurturing on your part. For years, I deceived myself into believing that I accepted my loss when I was really in denial. There were times when I'd resurface from the pain I was drowning in to relish in moments of peace, but those passing moments of rescue only lasted for so long. Before I knew it I was submerged under my own misery again. I finally made the decision to confront my loss. The first step to recovery is acknowledging your pain and coming face to face with whatever has you bound. For me, that meant accepting what happened to me as it was and coming out of the place of mourning and grieving.

Scripture tells us, "Blessed are those who mourn, for they will be comforted" (Matthew 5:4). You will never know God as a comforter if you never experience pain in life and allow Him to comfort you. There is no such thing as a pain free life and we can't live life avoiding pain, so we must prepare for it instead. I know firsthand that there is danger in unresolved pain. Internalizing pain can result in your body expressing your grief in other forms such as stress, headaches, weight gain, weight loss, hair loss and a variety of other symptoms. What you fail to express taking place internally, will eventually manifest itself externally. My body became my worst enemy, I always felt like I was going to die. I feared that one day I would be permanently disabled and my husband and daughter would have to care for me. I had multiple scares and issues that landed me in emergency rooms, doctor's offices, and even under the knife, again. From lumps in my breast, to hypoglycemic episodes that nearly caused me to pass out, joint pain, to discovering I had polycystic ovarian syndrome and a cyst the size of a golf ball on the only ovary I had left. I ended up having it removed.

By the grace of God, I've never experienced an injury like having a broken bone, but I do know that the first thing the doctor usually asks a patient is, "Are you in any pain?" and if so, "Where?" They'll even ask, "On a scale of 1 to 10 how bad is your pain?" Now, if I walked into an emergency room bleeding profusely with a broken bone piercing through my skin it would be foolish of me to tell the doctor I wasn't in any pain. Obviously, I'd be in pain or would be by the time the adrenaline wore off. On the other hand, if I had a condition in which my pain was not clearly evident, the only way the doctor would be able to understand the severity is by asking questions. "How much does it hurt? Where does it hurt? When did it start?" You're wondering what I'm trying to say, right? It's simple. Open up your mouth! Talking to someone about your pain is imperative to getting the help and treatment you need! Yes, even if that means paying someone to tell all your business to then do it!

The good Lord blessed us with counselors, psychologists, and doctors for a reason. Practice using discernment or common sense and get help! Unresolved pain creates a challenge for the person dealing with it. I know it's not easy sharing your pain with someone who can't see or understand it, but it's worth a try. First, I encourage you to talk to God about your pain and condition because He is the best doctor, counselor, and healer for your spirit! Allow Him to lead you to whomever it is so that you can get the help you need in the natural. There is nothing wrong with seeking help from a professional! Finding your voice is important and finding someone to help you along the way is too.

The next step is understanding that you are not able to change what happened to you, but you must realize that God has given you the power to overcome and that He is willing to heal you. Being an overcomer means you have no choice but to become better. I had to release myself from being bound to myself to be cleansed from the pain, anger, resentment, bitterness and unforgiveness. **Denying yourself permission to be better only keeps you bitter.** I reached a point where I was tired of being the same! I WANTED to be healed and after failed attempts at trying to do it on my own I had no choice but to BELIEVE that God was able to heal me!

Healing can occur immediately or in stages. If you have the faith, just a simple touch or a spoken word from God can heal you, suddenly. In Matthew 8:1-3, a leper approached Jesus and said to Him, "Lord, if you are willing, you can heal me and make me clean. Jesus reached out and touched him and said, "I am willing, be healed"(NLT). Do you doubt that God is willing to heal you? I know I did. I lacked the faith that God was willing, even though I knew He was able. God is never reluctant to heal us, it's our hesitancy to ask for it. This leper was tired of being the way he was and he approached Jesus with a level of faith that enabled him to receive his healing, immediately!

Unlike this particular leper, my healing occurred over time and as I was obedient to God's commands. **There is healing in instructions.** In Luke 17:14 Jesus instructed ten men with leprosy, "Go show yourselves to the priests" And as they went, they were cleansed of their leprosy" (NLT). obedient! He instructed me to go, move, and do specific things I was afraid to do, but God was glorified through my obedience. The length of time you suffer and the method by which you are healed sometimes depends on your level of faith and the capacity in which God wants to use you after being healed. The higher the level God is calling you to serve in, the deeper He must go in to rebuild and lay the new foundation for you to stand upon. Hence, the more painful your healing process may be. No matter what, after being healed your response should be, "Lord I'll serve you."

I suffered from a loss in which I nor anyone else had control. I am unable to get back what was taken from me and it was only by the grace of God that I didn't lose my life or my child in the process. I avoided dealing with my grief because I was too consumed with concealing my shame. I carried on with my life thinking it wouldn't phase me because I was young and didn't want any more kids. I thought my majoring in Psychology would aid in my ability to "fix" myself, however, only a power greater could restore my spiritual, mental, and emotional health. It takes daily effort to defeat the work of depression and anxiety before the poison spreads uncontrollably. Some people resort to taking medication, to each his own. I'm not against it, but I don't fully understand the long-term benefit in taking medications with possible side-effects that can potentially create more problems. Yes, I have swallowed a pill a time or two out of desperation for sleep, comfort, and peace of mind, but I'm convinced that popping pills is not the best treatment for me. Plus, I don't like taking medicine! I believed that the Word of God was powerful enough to transform my mind and the mental ailments I was dealing with. I also believe that the word of God can be used in conjunction with pastoral or professional counseling.

Often, it requires more than a few scriptures or speaking positive affirmations for a person with anxiety to overcome it. Especially during the times when you can't find the strength to read or regurgitate the Word of God to combat the negative thoughts and emotions. If you struggle with anxiety or depression you must seek God's direction for your healing. Just know that you are not suffering alone. There are many Christian women like me, who have battled with or is still battling with anxiety and depression and it's not something to be ashamed of. In the bible, David wrote about his anguish, loneliness, sin, guilt, and fear of the enemy multiple times throughout the book of Psalms.

"Why are you downcast, oh my soul? Why so disturbed within me? Put your hope in God for I will yet praise Him, my Savior and my God" - Psalm. 42:11

Moses lived in hopelessness for 40 years, he didn't believe that he was worthy or that he could be used to fulfill God's plan. These beliefs are consistent with depression. God sent Moses to warn Pharaoh many times and Moses still complained to the Lord that Pharaoh wouldn't listen even though God had already told Moses it would happen that way. Still, God showed patience towards Moses until Moses saw his purpose restored by God. In the same way, you may believe the purpose in which God created you for is destroyed and beyond restoration. Remember, God is still able! He is waiting patiently for you to hear His voice, open your heart, and receive His call!

I used to worry about people viewing me differently once they knew about my struggle. Then it dawned on me that everyone is fighting a battle that no else knows about. We only allow people to see and know the things what we want them to. I had to own my pain instead of allowing it to own me. Instead of allowing my circumstances to keep me bound from my purpose, I chose to believe that in Romans 8:28, "all things work together for good to them that love God, to them who are called according to His purpose. (NLT)" If you ever want to become fruitful in life, experience growth, be influential, impactful, and empower others, you must get to the root of your own pain, own it, and decide NOT to let it destroy you. I made a decision to change my pain from a path of destruction to a path of strength. Strength training is all about resistance! It was time for me to put in the work required to obtain my healing.

The Struggle

Once you've opened up your heart to God and your mouth to whomever He leads you to for help, there's still more work to be done. With every step I made towards healing, the enemy tried to use my weaknesses to pull me back and make me feel as though I wasn't making progress. I came across another harsh reality that crying out to God and others about my pain was easy but, admitting the pain I caused others forced me to take a good look at myself in the mirror. I knew the time would come for me to have a much needed, long, overdue, and uncomfortable conversation with my husband about myself. I wasn't quite prepared for his response either.

I was perfect and could do no harm to others, so I thought! I was completely oblivious as to how much my attitude toward my husband affected him until he opened up and shared his heart with me. Eric came home from work one evening and I was sitting at the dining room table waiting to engage in conversation about US. Of course, I started expressing my feelings like always and how emotionally disconnected I felt from him. He became emotionally disconnected early on in our marriage, especially after multiple deployments to war. He'd seen and been through so much that I didn't know about. I knew expressing himself was an issue, but I was tired of him shutting me out emotionally and he was probably tired of me saying whatever I felt like all the time. I asked him why he wouldn't open up to me and his exact words were, "I feel like I'm a slave to you. Sometimes the way you look at me makes me feel... inadequate." He didn't understand how it felt to have a part of him missing, but hearing him say those words made me realize I'd accomplished the very thing I sought to do for years... make him feel my pain. He connected with the feeling of inadequacy without knowing it was how I defined myself. I'd never felt more toxic in my life before until that very moment. Every belief I had about me being a good person was shattered. *Ouch, that hurt God.* The saying, "Hurt people hurt people" was indeed true. Here I was thinking that I was only hurting myself, not only was I damaged and in need of healing, but he was too.

For years, I had been asking Eric to love me in a way that I wouldn't allow him to. Ephesians 5:28-29 implores husbands to "Love their wives as their own bodies. He who loves his wife loves himself. After all, no one ever hated their own body, but they feed and care for their body, just as Christ does the church" (NIV). I realized the role I played in damaging his heart and how it contributed to not only the way he loved me but himself as well I was not content with his love for me because it was always a reflection of how I loved myself. I made him feel unworthy of love, grace, and forgiveness by silently making him pay for the things I suffered from that was in no way his fault. Yet, he remained steady with me and was right there loving me the best way he knew how. It takes a strong person to love you through your mess. I couldn't see it back then but, the scales were removed from my eyes and I realized how Eric displayed Christ's love for me more than I ever did for him. Regardless of how much I tried to change him or what I did to hurt him, he always loved me, accepted me, and affirmed me.

As God heals you he will shed light on your blind spots and reveal the things you fail to see or admit about yourself. Very often we do things that nurture our pain instead of neutering it and we end up hurting others in the process. You may be embarrassed by the fruit your bitter seeds produce, but to remedy the fruit you have to address the root. Unforgiveness was one fruit that I needed to uproot.

For years I told myself that I forgave Eric but I still felt the negative emotions whenever I thought about the past or looked him in the eye. I realized it wasn't my failure to forgive him that became a stumbling block for my healing process but forgiving myself was the real issue. Forgiveness is for you, not for the person who hurt you. Many of us sit back and sip on poison while waiting for the other person to die when the very person you resent for hurting you has no idea about your pain! Those people are usually content, enjoying, and living life while you're stuck being miserable! If you can relate, you are bound to yourself! Be free! Let it go! There's no point in wanting freedom if you refuse to let go of your pain!

Letting Go

The fear of letting go is another issue I had to uproot. After feeling like I'd lost so much, letting go of anything I attached myself to became even more difficult. I used to think that letting go was a sign of weakness. So not true! Running away may be viewed as a sign of weakness depending on the situation; however, it often takes more strength to let go of something than it does to hold on to it. A level of your spiritual maturity is determined by your ability to let go. Life is filled with a never-ending series of letting go, from the moment we are born we were conditioned to let go. **God won't rescue you from the things you refuse to relinquish to Him.**

I used to struggle with letting go anything I worked hard to obtain in my life: security, my accomplishments, possessions, friends, and even my credit score! Letting go of people and my need for security has always been the toughest task for me. It takes a lot for me to let others into my heart, but once you're in, you're in. It's that much more difficult for me to let someone go after I've designated a space in my heart for them. For some reason, when I must let go of people it feels like they're taking my intellectual property away with them. Have you ever wanted to take back all that you've given and poured into someone after they've misused, abused, or dismissed your loyalty as a way of saying "thank you"? God wants to loose you from a life of pleasing people and lead you to living a life that solely pleases Him. If He has to remove certain individuals from your life to do so, He will do it. Sometimes, people will disappear for you, other times, you'll have to cut ties instead of trying to force them into a space where there's not enough room to accommodate them.

Throughout your healing process you must realize that everyone won't grow with you and can't go where God is taking you. You must be okay with that! When God told Abraham in Genesis 12:1-14 to leave his land, relatives, and his father's house to go to a land He would show him, Abraham went with his wife, herdsmen, tents, and flocks, but he also took his nephew Lot with him. Lot also brought his flocks, herds, and tents along with him and eventually they came to a place where the land they dwelled in couldn't accommodate or sustain both of their livestock together.

Strife stirred up among them and Abraham asked Lot to leave. He told him he could go and inhabit whatever land he laid his eyes on. Lot's eyes saw the valley of Jordan, which was a land well-watered and wanted by Abraham. They parted ways and Abraham kept on going, discouraged because he thought he'd lost the land promised to him. However, AFTER Lot had separated from Abraham, God showed Abraham all the lands from the north, south, east and west that He would give to him and his decedents forever. Abraham thought he had lost the best land, but what Lot ended up inhabiting was the land of Sodom and Gomorrah, a land that was ultimately destroyed. If that story doesn't make it clear for you let me say it loud and clear! You'll have a LOT to lose on your way to your destiny, that includes your negative thinking, bad habits, behaviors, ex's, friends, and as Abraham learned the hard way, sometimes your own kinfolk GOT TO GO! The moment you feel like you're giving up your "best" for something you perceive as less, just remember that we serve a God who likes to add and multiply after what seems like a subtraction taking place in your life!

How often have you fought to hold onto something out of fear that there's nothing better for you? How often have you lived in the past instead of grabbing a hold of your future? Letting go is such a daunting task, but why? I realized that the fear of letting go is rooted in having little faith. When we desperately hold onto something God wants us to let go of, what we're really saying to Him is, "I don't believe you have something better for me." So, we end up settling for less than God's best. Settling for less is really operating in disobedience!

Take a moment and examine the areas in your life where you're living in disobedience because you've refused to let go. Consider the number of friendships, relationships, blessings, opportunities, exhilarating experiences, and prosperous years you've missed out on all because you refused to let go. Please beloved, don't let your destiny pass you by another day! Once you master the art of letting go, your faith will grow and GO to the next level. Letting go ultimately teaches you to trust God. I wanted to trust God, but I needed to be delivered from my pained, perfect self!

Little Miss Perfect

I am a very strategic person who likes making plans and paying attention to every little detail. I don't take pride in things being half done and I refuse to accept anything less than perfection. I enjoyed thinking that being a perfectionist served me well; especially as a student or an employee. I always aimed to please others and myself because it gave me a sense of pride.

Depending on others to do something right for me is still somewhat difficult. You know the old saying, "if you want something done right the first time, you have to do it yourself?" Well, that's me. If you are a perfectionist like me, we tend to have expectations and standards for ourselves that we won't always hold others to. Everyone else can make the mistakes that you can't. Can you relate? If so, you'll learn the hard way that being a perfectionist can be very stressful, damaging, and unhealthy for you and for others. The ugly truth about being a perfectionist is that it's a more deeply rooted issue than most people understand. It's an insecurity rooted in fear and the desire to please others.

Fear and the need to please others took root early on in my childhood as I explained earlier in my book. My desire to be better, have more and give my family a better life placed a heavy burden on me to outperform myself and others just for approval. I realized that the fear of failing, not being good enough, and wanting to make everyone else happy at the expense of my own happiness would never make me *perfect*. It only made me more flawed.

Being a perfectionist is a cover up to disguise your inadequacies. I'm still learning how to let go the idea of perfection because it doesn't exist. **Perfection is the perfect deception,** it's a sensation or feeling that no human on earth will ever attain. There's nothing wrong with having high standards, in fact, we should all develop a spirit of excellence, but let go of your need to be perfect. When you do, you will embrace the liberty that comes with being who you are rather than being a slave to the person you aren't. If you want to be transformed, you must first come to terms with your true self. Surrendering a false version of who you are for a better pseudo version of yourself won't do you any good. Don't resist changing, embrace it!

Metamorphosis

"A change of the form or nature of a thing or person into a completely different one, by natural or supernatural means."

My outward appearance began changing, but it was the transformation taking place on the inside that no one could see. Transformation is a rewarding, but difficult process! Let me be the first to tell you, it hurts like hell! It isn't easy or comfortable and it certainly doesn't happen overnight! I went through some serious renovations in my heart, mind, body, and spirit. I'm still a work in progress, but I'll never forget the struggle.

I'm reminded of the Israelites and how they were exiled from their land and held captive for seventy years because God removed His presence from them. Their sin, stubbornness, and rebellion caused their hearts to be hardened towards God. Even though He promised to restore them and the land, they had to endure longsuffering. Their time of suffering served as a reminder admonishing them not to turn back to their ways that displeased God. In Ezekiel 36:26 God told them, "And I will give you a new heart, and a new spirit I will put in you. And I will remove the heart of stone from your flesh and give you a heart of flesh." (NLT). What felt like punishment to the Israelites was actually God performing heart surgery and giving them a new, undivided heart towards Him.

For years, I held onto pain, anger and resentment towards my husband and God. What I considered punishment was actually a lesson God used to perform heart surgery on me. I walked around believing my pain made me strong, but the reality is it made my heart cold. As I surrendered to God, I embraced being vulnerable, and allowed the Holy Spirit to transform me, I realized my true source of strength. 2 Corinthians 12:9 (NLT) says, "My grace is all you need. My power works best in weakness…" I can declare that, "I am glad to boast about my weaknesses, so that the power of Christ can work through me."

As God began to transform me from the inside out, I couldn't help but relate my journey to the remarkable metamorphosis of a butterfly. If you've never studied a caterpillar's transformation into a butterfly, allow me to give you a quick lesson! The Webster's dictionary defines metamorphosis as: "A change of physical form, structure, or substance especially by supernatural means. A striking alteration in appearance, character, or circumstances. A typically marked and abrupt developmental change in the form or structure of an animal occurring subsequent to birth or hatching."

First, I'm seriously not a huge fan of insects, I cringe, jump and scream at the sight of spiders, roaches, worms, bugs, whatever you can think of, I don't like them. I just don't understand their purpose and don't care to know sometimes. With that being said, caterpillars are insects. As a little girl, I hated walking down the street and over to my grandma Audrey's house during the spring because the trees would be covered with caterpillars! The tree trunks, branches, and leaves were saturated with black worms that would fall into my head as I dashed for the front door! I absolutely hated them. Oddly, as an adult I became extremely fond of butterflies. In fact, the only tattoo I have on my body is that of a butterfly. Granted, I probably won't ever get another one, but if I did, guess what it would be? Yep, a butterfly. Butterflies are unique, rare, and very delicate, but a butterfly is not just born a butterfly; it is born a caterpillar! *Does a caterpillar know it's going to eventually become a butterfly? Does the butterfly remember it was once a caterpillar? What all takes place in the cocoon?* These are some of the questions I pondered.

I discovered the life cycle of a butterfly consists of four stages: Egg, Larva, Pupa, and the Adult stage. Each stage has a different purpose. Of course, the butterfly starts life as a small egg, when the egg hatches the small caterpillar is born and immediately starts its work. The Larva stage (caterpillar) is all about growth. The caterpillar starts eating the leaf it was born on and will even eat its shell as it contains nourishment that's beneficial to its growth.[1] Eating is the caterpillar's main focus. Must be nice, right? But, there's a reason it has to eat so much.

During this stage, the caterpillar needs enough food to sustain itself through the next stage. Without the proper nourishment, it may not have the energy to complete its metamorphosis. As the caterpillar grows it sheds several times. A caterpillar's skin doesn't stretch, so molting is its way of shedding skin to accommodate its growing size. When the caterpillar reaches its full length and mass it hangs upside down on a tree and forms itself into a pupa (cocoon).[1] The pupa stage, also known as chrysalis or cocoon, is my favorite! "Why is that," you ask? I'll tell you. Looking from the outside, the caterpillar appears to be good and resting, but inside is where the struggle is taking place! Inside the cocoon the caterpillar wraps itself in a fluid-like substance where its body and wings dissolve and breakdown into the fluid. The caterpillar's body is changing; relinquishing one form for another in order to emerge.[1] Metamorphosis is a beautiful mystery, it's a process that involves struggle that often goes unnoticed. There's a story I found that I want to share with you:

"There was a gardener who was out tending his garden one day and observed a butterfly struggling to break free of its cocoon. The gardener watched in amazement as the delicate creature struggled violently to work its way out of its constraining space. The entire cocoon shook and trembled with the butterfly's efforts to emerge. This struggle went on for what seemed like an eternity to the concerned gardener. Eventually, the gardener became so distraught over the butterfly's wrestling to break free that he lost patience and decided to help the process along. He went into the house and obtained a pair of scissors, returned to the garden and cut a larger opening in the wall of the cocoon, allowing the butterfly to tumble out onto the ground. What the well-meaning gardener did not realize is that the struggle is part of the transformation process. In the cocoon, the young butterfly's wings are engorged with fluid, and the struggle to emerge from the cocoon forces the fluid out of the wings and into the young creature's body where it can be

161

absorbed and processed. Deprived of part of its transformative process, this particular butterfly's wings remained fluid-filled and it was never able to fly. The gardener watched in despair as the butterfly slowly died, lying on the ground in his garden."

- Unknown Author

Practical Application

There are many lessons we can learn from this story and from the life cycle of the butterfly that can be applied to your own spiritual transformation. In your caterpillar stage, it is imperative that you get nourished with the word of God, grow in wisdom, understanding and in strength in order to sustain you throughout your transformation. God began feeding and preparing me in seasons prior to the struggle I encountered that lead me to writing this book. Throughout my process I fed on the word that was already hidden in my heart, but my hunger and thirst for more caused me to dig deeper into God's word. Malnourished caterpillars may become butterflies, but risk the inability to reproduce![1] That message alone will preach itself! You may be wondering like I did, *what if you never make it to your "cocoon stage?" What happens to the caterpillars that don't transform?*

Of course, the first thing that came to my mind was they get stomped on by humans or eaten by birds. (*Not like I'm guilty of doing such a thing...Father forgive me for all those times I stomped on the chubby caterpillars. I understand their purpose now and promise not to ever do it again. In Jesus' name, Amen.*) Don't judge me. Anyway, caterpillars aren't at the top of the food chain, which means they are preyed upon, however, they are very creative when it comes to self-defense! Caterpillars have the ability to take on the color or form of their environment. They know how to blend in with plants and trees and they can make themselves visible with bright colors to advertise how toxic they are.[2] This tactic prevents the birds from eating them. Caterpillars eat plants that contain toxins their bodies can tolerate, yet are deadly to its predator. The brighter the colors on a butterfly, the more toxic it is![2] I bet you didn't know that! Whew, God gave me a revelation of a difference about that! I'm about to start preaching!

Looking at this from a spiritual view, your environment is crucial to your survival during your process! You must be intentional about protecting your peace because spiritual warfare is inevitable once you submit to God's transforming power! The enemy formulates strategies to disturb your peace and bring about turmoil. He will utilize people, problems, pain, and pressure to abort your process! The gardener in the story didn't realize that the struggle was essential to the caterpillars process of becoming a butterfly. Although he meant no harm, his lack of knowledge and understanding caused him to end the butterfly's process before its time. The lesson in this is that people can thwart your progression or work against God's purpose for your life because they are jealous, envious, or simply don't understand your struggle! For instance, have you ever had someone "advise" or try to talk you out of a season of struggle God intended for you to endure, knowing that the struggle was meant to develop and teach you discipline? Maybe you've been betrayed or manipulated out of your purpose by friends or family members who don't want you to receive God's blessings? Pray and ask God to help you discern people's motives because the enemy will use anything and anybody to destroy your purpose! The last thing Satan wants is for you to become a driving force for the Kingdom of God. So, be careful who you fellowship with during your metamorphosis because not everyone is going to nourish or foster your process. There is healing in the right fellowship and you can't afford to break bread with people who are fixed on being jealous, broken, busted, and disgusted the rest of their lives.

I'm not saying that God can't use you to minister to broken people during this season in your life but, if you are lacking the faith and spiritual strength to carry the weight of the warfare that comes along with it, then don't. I recommend you surround yourself with people who will nurture and speak life to you during your process rather than remaining in familiar environments that make you feel vulnerable.

Don't get distracted by the detours the enemy will throw at you. The devil has studied you and has specifically assigned demons to take you out! But you must "Put on the full armor of God, so that you can take your stand against the devil's schemes. For our struggle is not against flesh and blood, but against the rulers, against authorities, against the powers of this dark world and against the spiritual forces of evil in the heavenly realms" (Ephesians 6:10-18 NIV). The Word of God tells us to stand firm with the belt of truth buckled around our waist, with the breastplate of righteousness in place, and with our feet planted in the gospel of peace. We must take up the shield of faith to stop the fiery arrows of the devil, take on the helmet of salvation and the sword of the spirit, which is the word of God. "The weapons may form against you, but they will NOT prosper," according to Isaiah 54:17. The Word of God is the "toxin" you'll need to protect you. Your body can tolerate it but it's deathly to predators of darkness!

Take advantage of your caterpillar stage. Eat! Grow! Then eat and grow some more! Get so fat on the Word of God to where Christ's light shines so bright from within you!

Renewing of The Mind

The renewing of your mind occurs in your "pupa" or "cocoon" stage and is also crucial to your survival. The Holy Spirit comes in to sweep clean, burn away, refine, and rid your mind of old beliefs, lies, and thoughts because 2 Corinthians 5:17 says, "If any man be in Christ, he is a new creature; old things are passed away; behold, all things are become new" (KJV). Then Romans 12:2 warns us not to "copy the behavior and customs of this world, but let God transform you into a new person by changing the way you think. Then you will learn to know God's will for you, which is good and pleasing and perfect"(NLT).

The way you think must be changed because your thoughts control your choices, your choices control your actions, and your actions determine your outcomes. It makes no sense to become a butterfly if you're going to continue thinking, acting and living like a caterpillar! Butterflies don't crawl they fly high and see things from a totally different perspective than the caterpillar. Renewing your mind with the Word of God enables you to see things from His perspective (things above) and not your own limited view (things beneath). I dived head first into God's word and intentionally sought scriptures to help me get through this phase. For every lie the enemy told me regarding my mind, my worth, my freedom, my peace, trusting God and overcoming fear, I went and found a direct scripture, truth, and promise of God that contradicted it. Here are a few scriptures I referenced in each area:

Renewing the Mind
Romans 8:22, Titus 1:15, 1 Corinthians 2:6, James 1:6-8

Worth/Self Esteem
Philippians 4:13, 1 Corinthians 6:19, Psalm 28:76, 46:5; Romans 5:8; 1 Thessalonians 1:4, Colossians 2:10, Isaiah 62:4

Freedom
Romans 8:1, John 8:36, Galatians 5:1, Ephesians 3:12; Acts 13:38-39, Colossians 1: 21-23

Peace
Philippians 4:7, John 14:27

Trusting God
Psalms 37: 4-5, 56:3; 1 Peter 1:21; 5:7; Deuteronomy 31:6, Matthew 28:20

Worry/Fear
Isaiah 41:10, Luke 12:11, Matthew 6:34, Proverbs 12:25

You will respond differently to people, problems, pressures and pain when you learn to apply the truth of God's word in your life. God renews your spirit and cleans you up on the inside so that others can see HIS glory upon you on the outside! All that you once were and all that you will be is embodied within the cocoon, the place of struggle. But you must willingly surrender the form of the caterpillar in order to take on the form of the butterfly. Don't be resistant, but expect resistance!

Growing Pains

Amiyah was around the age of five-years-old when she started having these horrible aches in her legs. The pain would usually come after doing some type of extracurricular activity for a long period of time such as running, climbing, or jumping around. The pain affected her in both legs; starting in the front of her thighs and working its way down to her knees and calves. There were times at night when she would wake up out of her sleep crying frantically, "mommy my legs hurt!" To see the agonizing pain in her eyes was unbearable. I felt helpless not being able to take her pain away, I opted to give her Tylenol or anything that would help to ease the pain, but it didn't help much. I would massage and pray silently over her legs until the pain subsided.

One night we were sitting in Bible Study and the aching started again. She suffered, silently, but somehow managed to make it until the end of service. After being dismissed we stopped to say goodnight to a friend of mine. Meanwhile, one of the women in the church, who just so happened to be a nurse, noticed Amiyah crying and came over to check on her. She wrapped Amiyah in her arms and gently rubbed her hand across her back as Amiyah told her about the pain she was feeling. I explained to the woman, whose name I do not know to this day, how often the pains occurred. Based on the information I gave her she assumed it was growing pangs. To be certain, she advised me to mention it to our primary care physician the next time Amiyah had an appointment.

On another occasion, Amiyah and I were out having lunch at her favorite restaurant-Cheddars. When the pain started in her leg a waitress noticed her crying and saw me massaging her leg under the table. The waitress came over and sat down beside Amiyah. She informed me that she was a graduate student and was studying Kinesiology. She mentioned how every now and then the leg muscles ache and cramp as they are growing. She advised me to feed Amiyah more potassium-rich foods. Then she went to the kitchen and brought back a small amount of pickle juice for Amiyah to drink. Apparently, there is something in pickle juice that helps relieve cramps. I'm sure it might have worked had Amiyah been able to drink it without nearly vomiting all over the place. Eventually, I took Amiyah to the doctor to see what was going on.

After describing what her symptoms were the doctor's diagnosis was "Yep, you guessed it right-growing pains!" The doctor informed us that the pain would come and go throughout her childhood and possibly even throughout her teenage years. Unfortunately, there was no treatment or prescription drug to eliminate her growing pains. This was just a stage that her body just had to go through. In my mind, this was only the beginning of the many growing pains she would experience in life. The same applies to the growing pains in my life and yours, I found out the hard way that if you want the promise of a pain free life-there isn't one. Pain is inevitable, but it doesn't have to be disabling. There are seasons when God will stretch you beyond your comfort zone. God will even take the very thing that makes you comfortable and use it to position you in a place where He can make you uncomfortable all for His glory. Remember, even during the pain something beautiful is taking place...growth.

Amiyah and I tend to have some of our most deep conversations while driving around together. One night on our way home from me-ma and papa's house, which is where she loves spending most of her time, I mentioned that her dad and I decided that we would all go visit another local church that upcoming Sunday. I told her the name of the church and she said, "Mom, I don't want to go to that church, it's not all that good." "Why do you say that?" I asked. The last time we visited this church was when she was about two years old and something happened during service that rubbed me the wrong way. Amiyah was too young to understand what happened that day and I didn't make it a point to tell her about it as she got older. Yet, at the age of 10 here she was giving me her opinion about the same church. She then told me that some of her friends had visited the church and weren't too fond of it. Therefore, her opinion was based on their judgment. I immediately jumped on this opportunity to teach her a little something about life. "Amiyah, you can't go through life making decisions or forming opinions about someone or something based on what others say or think," I told her. She was immediately offensive and tried justifying what she had just said. I implored her to just listen to me for a moment. I explained to her that everyone else's perception isn't everything. Sometimes she must experience some things and get to know some people for herself, first, before passing judgment or forming blind opinions. In the middle of this deep, heart-to-heart conversation Amiyah proceeded to cry. "Why are you crying", I asked her, "tell me what's on your mind." With tears rolling down her face she whispered, "I'm just afraid of growing up in life and the thought of not always having you around to help me scares me."

You know that lump you get in your throat that creates a burning sensation right as you're about to start crying? Yeah, I had one of those moments. With a glossy look in my eyes and with a faint voice I expressed, "I'll always be there for you baby, no matter what." As a mother, it's only natural for me to want to protect my child from certain things in life. I don't want her to make the same mistakes I made or to experience some of the hurts, heartaches, and pains I did. I can't guarantee her a life filled without pain, but I can guarantee that I'll be right there with her through it all.

Things Happen Naturally

I remember another time Amiyah and I were leaving the dentist office after having her tooth pulled. Little did she know, I was struggling to find encouragement that I needed myself at that moment. I asked her if she had anything inspirational to share with me. Of course, after explaining what inspiration meant and helping her understand what I was asking of her, with a numb mouth, full of gauze and drool she responded, "Oh yes! I have something for you". Eager to listen, I turned down the music on the radio and waited for her response. "Have no fear, some things in life are just meant to happen naturally...like growing up". I looked at her and smiled. Those were exactly the words I needed to hear. *Some things are just meant to happen naturally.*

It warmed my heart to hear her utter those words, bearing in mind the last conversation we had while driving home. I'd been dealing with a few fears of my own as I was in another transition point in my life. My fear was that I'd never become the person I knew God called me to be. I was afraid that I didn't have what it would take to carry out the vision God gave me and to achieve my goals. I was even more afraid of everything not turning out the right way. But, her quote challenged my perspective. I began to reflect on how fear sets in to distract us from accomplishing things in life that God has already determined are going to happen in due time.

If you've ever experienced the fear of the unknown, the fear of death, fear of failure, or in my case experiencing the fear of achieving success beyond your wildest imagination, then you can relate. Amiyah's fear of growing up wasn't going to keep her from growing up. For most people growing up, physically, is a natural process that occurs whether we want it to or not. It dawned on me that my fear of things going the wrong way in life isn't going to make them go right. Fear will always be present when you're taking a risk at something great. Whatever it is you desire to do in life that scares you feel the fear, prepare for the resistance, and do it anyway.

Meeting Resistance

As your mind is being transformed and you begin loving and seeing yourself the way God sees you, be prepared to meet resistance. Proverbs 4: 20-22 advises us to pay attention and listen carefully to God's word. "Don't lose sight of them. Let them penetrate deep into your heart for they bring life to those who find them and healing to their whole body." Then it cautions us in verse 23 to, "Guard your heart above all else, for it determines the course of your life."

You must guard your heart and mind from the enemy and people! Not everyone will be glad about your transformation and the devil sure as hell won't be! Some will question why you're so distant, why you don't do the things you used to do for them, why you act like you're "too good" or "better" than them. They won't agree with the decisions you make or what you have to say at times! People will literally STOP liking you for no reason! Your transformation will cause a great deal of people to feel uncomfortable around you! Why? Because your submission and obedience to God creates a heightened sensitivity in others about their resistance and disobedience to Him. Nevertheless, keep moving forward and growing in Christ.

Growth reveals treasures about you that comfort conceals. Your growth reveals who is really for you and who is against you. People are fine with you when you're bound and miserable, but have a problem with you when you're free! But it's not completely their

176

fault, if they understood your struggle then maybe they would appreciate your transformation a bit more!

Your transformation might seem even more painful than just remaining the same! You definitely will experience a crushing like never before as God chips away the stone from your heart, shines light on the dark places of your soul, and renews a right mind and spirit within you. Labor pains aren't any fun when a mother is birthing a baby, in the end the joy of holding a sweet little miracle makes it so worth it! You must endure new pain to process the old pain! You can make it! You have no other choice but to make it through if you want to be healed and restored!

Healed & Restored

I held on to my pain as tightly as I could and I refused to break free from its grasp. I had my share of pleasant moments and encountered many beautiful spirits along the way that were fundamental to my growth and healing. One experience I'd like to share with you happened during the weekend of my daughter's fourteenth birthday. Celebrating her day was always bittersweet for me because I was reminded of the joy and pain I experienced. Amiyah allowed me to miss her birthday this year to attend a Writer's Retreat in Orlando so that I could work on this book.

The day of her birthday I found myself extremely overwhelmed with gratefulness to the point of tears. I was in my room and the Spirit of God fell on me so heavily that all I could do was cry and worship! I felt grateful for God allowing me to witness another year of my daughter's life and I was simply thankful to be alive! This was a feeling I never sensed before. I called my daughter, sung happy birthday to her and told her how much I loved her! I then had the opportunity to share my testimony with a beautiful spirit by the name of Karolyne Roberts, the CEO and Founder of The Writer's Retreat. After giving her the quick version of my story and leaving some information out, she opened up her mouth and confirmed the exact words God spoke to my spirit years ago. "You may not give birth in the natural again, but spiritually you'll birth many". I started crying as I shared with her that God spoke those exact words to me in the past.

That Sunday, I left the retreat and headed to church where my husband and I were confirmed and ordained into ministry. That same evening, I was invited to attend a memorial ceremony at the hospital I gave birth at. Let me remind you, I hadn't stepped foot into this place since the day I was discharged years ago. Exhausted, but longing to show my support, I mustered up the strength to go and I took Amiyah with me. So, we went to the place where it all began exactly fourteen years and two days ago. The ceremony was for women and families who suffered the tragic loss of a baby either during their pregnancy or at birth.

As we approached the outside garden at the hospital, I heard a familiar voice speaking and giving words of encouragement from the podium. The closer we got to the setting the more I recognized the voice and the frame of the individual speaking. "That sounds like the doctor who delivered you and performed my surgery," I whispered to Amiyah. I opened the program that was handed to me and found the physician's name listed as the speaker. Amiyah and I took seats up in the front behind my friend and her family. After the doctor was done speaking, she stepped down from the podium and sat directly in front me in the row ahead.

I sat there glaring at her and feeling somewhat indifferent as the painful memories and countless thoughts raced through my mind. I thought about introducing myself and asking her questions to see if she remembered me. *Will she answer my questions? Did she really do everything she could that day to stop the bleeding? Should I share all the pain I've been through since she made the decision to take my womb?* I was confused and perplexed as to what I'd say to her, if I should say anything at all. I focused my attention back on the podium and listened as the grieving parents took turns sharing their painful stories. I couldn't help but notice a spirit of heaviness on the doctor as they poured their hearts out. I noticed how her eyes stuck to the ground, her body sat uncomfortably in the chair, how she fought back tears as images of the lifeless babies flashed across the projector screen.

During a moment of silence, we were given candles to light in memory of the little angels that had passed. As I sat there with my candle lit, the Holy Spirit immediately quickened me to speak to the doctor. *"Huh? You want me to say something to her God? You don't want me to do that!! What am I going to say?"* This is how the conversation went in my head, I was hesitant at first, but He kept leading me to speak! Not knowing what to say, I obeyed and swiftly called out her name.

The doctor turned around and looked me right in the eyes. I then pointed to Amiyah, opened up my mouth and whispered to the doctor, "Fourteen years ago you delivered THIS gift!" Amiyah looked at her, smiled and waved in excitement. I watched as the doctor's countenance lifted, and a heartwarming smile adorned her face as her eyes focused on Amiyah for a brief moment. "Her!" she said softly. Without saying another word, she simply smiled and waved back at Amiyah, then I got up and walked away. I went to the back of the garden that was lit with butterflies my friend had spread throughout the grounds the day before. As I read over the names of the babies engraved in the stone statues I wondered if I would ever run into the doctor again. I didn't.

The next morning as I was laying in my bed, I had some one on one time with God. I asked Him, if it was by chance that after all these years I finally had an encounter with that doctor. The strange part was that I finally had the opportunity to share my pain with her, but I just couldn't. God is so intentional. I questioned *"Why God? Why on the third day after my daughters 14th birthday would you allow this to happen?"* Just as clear as day He replied, *"I needed YOU to be revived."*

As I reflected on our short encounter, I considered the environment we were in and suddenly things made sense. I thought about the precious lives delivered that didn't survive and the numerous amount of times the doctor has had to deliver heartbreaking news to mothers, fathers, and families. I literally felt the heaviness of her burden fall upon me. An extremely sorrowful burden this doctor didn't ask for, but naturally comes with the territory of her job. The doctor was powerless in choosing whether or not those precious babies would live or die. Their destiny had already been predestined by God. Then I thought about the one decision the doctor did make fourteen years ago that changed my life. I realized there could have been two lives lost that day I gave birth, if those doctors hadn't delivered Amiyah as quickly as possible she could have suffocated in my blood. Then again, if the doctor didn't perform the hysterectomy to prevent me from bleeding out, I could have easily slipped away from time into eternity. But we both SURVIVED.

In an environment surrounded by heartache and pain, that night God used me to become a beacon of light. He tested and proved me to myself, that I was ready to be used. My focus shifted from my pain to my purpose, I was healed and ready to be restored!

Restored

Restoration is defined as the "act of returning something to a former owner, place, or condition." It is the process of repairing or rebuilding something so as to restore it to its original condition, if not better. Something must be lost or a loss must occur before restoration happens. Spiritual restoration is a process by which we are made whole again after a loss. If you know anything about renovating or restoring a home after it's been damaged then you might understand how the promise of restoration sounds good, but the process doesn't always feel good. In the book of Isaiah we find where God removed His presence from the Israelites and they were exiled from their land due to their sin and rebellion. Their land was deemed desolate and they were forsaken for a season, however, God promised that He would restore them and their land.

They suffered seventy years of captivity and chastisement, but it was for their own benefit. What felt like punishment was actually a lesson and preparation for what God had in store for them. You see, the Israelites needed to be reminded of who they were and who they belonged to. They were marked and chosen by God. He had to prune, refine, cleanse, change, and perform heart surgery on them before restoring them to their land and relationship with Him. God had to fill them with breath and life again for His name sake and to show them and the unbelievers His glory! I want you to understand this love, God is willing and able to heal and restore you after a devastating loss. The process isn't always easy, but it's necessary and all for the glory of God!

I asked God why it took fourteen years for me to receive my complete healing? He told me it was because I chose to hold on to the pain for that long and because I didn't have faith that He could heal me. I also understand that God works in time and seasons and according to Ecclesiastes 3:11, "He has made everything beautiful in its time"(NLT). I am one of those people who appreciate the meaning of things and biblical numerology captivates me. So, can you guess what my favorite number is? Nope, it's not the number fourteen. It's actually seven! My favorite number is seven, which biblically represents "completion OR perfection" both spiritually and naturally. Fourteen represents "deliverance" and is a multiple of the number seven. Stay with me, I promise I'm going somewhere with this! Fourteen being double the number seven implies a "DOUBLE PORTION OF SPIRUTAL PERFECTION!" The Lord declared to me Joel 2:25 that says, "I will give you back what you lost to the swarming locusts, the hopping locusts, the stripping locusts, and the cutting locusts" (NLT).

For the natural womb taken from me, God is giving me a double womb in the spirit! For all the years of peace, laughter, growth, joy, missed opportunities, hurt, lack, and struggle I endured, for everything that the swarming locusts consumed from me God is restoring and giving me a double portion! I believe it! I receive it! I claim it in Jesus' name!

By the time you finish reading this book, my husband and I will have celebrated approximately 24 years of being "together" and the renewal of our vows on our 13th year wedding anniversary. We've shared plenty of beautiful moments throughout our journey together so far; however, my hardened heart kept me from experiencing the true fullness of joy in my marriage. A space in my heart that was once bound and occupied by bitterness, clutter, and chaos, has now been loosed, cleaned, filled with love, sweet joy, gratefulness, respect, honor, and order. I can truly say that I love and respect my husband as the head of our home with all of my heart. When he changed my last name years ago I only gave him HALF of me. Now he has ALL of me; mind, body, and spirit. He's not just my soulmate, he's my spirit mate.

No, I'm not perfect. I still have my moments and days where I find myself sliding back into old habits and ways, but I don't stay there. Our marriage isn't perfect, but we're constantly making progress. We've been through so much together, we've grown closer, our love has evolved, and our relationship, trust and faith in God is more secure than before. I fought for my deliverance, healing, and transformation! I may have a slight limp, but I'm walking into my purpose! I am a NEW THING and God has given me a new name: DAUGHTER OF ZION.

Walking in Purpose

"The Spirit of the Lord God is upon Me, because the Lord has anointed me to preach good tidings to the poor; He has sent me to heal the brokenhearted, to proclaim liberty to the captives, and the opening of the prison to those who are bound; to proclaim the acceptable year of the Lord, And the day of vengeance of our God; to comfort all who mourn, to console those who mourn in Zion, to give them beauty for ashes, the oil of joy for mourning, the garment of praise for the spirit of heaviness; that they may be called trees of righteousness, the planting of the Lord, that He may be glorified."

- Isaiah 61: 1-3

My loss was shattering and the pain was great. Although, I allowed my circumstances to define me and make me feel desolate, I now understand that I was not forsaken by God. He was always there. I didn't always appreciate my worth as a caterpillar because I was deceived into thinking that I had no purpose or value. Do you know what caterpillars use to form their cocoons? SILK! They have the ability to produce something so precious and beautiful that can be used for a variety of things. Beloved, your pain may not feel good or even seem beautiful TO YOU, but it is **SILK TO SOMEONE ELSE.**

Your pain can run you straight into your destiny if you don't let it ruin you! I can hear some of you saying, "I don't know what my purpose is in life." If you don't know WHAT your purpose is let me help make it clearer: You were created to produce and bring glory to God! The butterfly's purpose is to reproduce and continue the life cycle. There is no glory in transforming into a butterfly that can't fulfill its purpose! I want you to just think about that for a moment...God has a special purpose just for you! No one else can do it like you or in the capacity that God has given you to do it.

Discovering what God's purpose is for your life can be challenging, but the only way you'll ever know what you were created for is by asking The Creator. This requires you to spend time at the feet of God, become in tune with yourself, discover your likes, dislikes, passions, and desires! A caterpillar understands its purpose and doesn't waste time moping around complaining about what it is as opposed to what it should be. These unique creatures understand the cycle of transformation and knows that The Creator did not design it to stay that way! You may not feel beautiful, worthy, or confident in the current state you are in, but rest assured knowing that you have a Heavenly Father who loves you too much to leave you the way you are!

He will transform you into something even more beautiful for HIS glory! Stand on God's promise and be confident in this: "He who began a good work in you will carry it on to completion until the day of Christ Jesus" (Philippians 1:6). Stop looking for your purpose in irrelevant people, places, things and opportunities and know that your sole purpose is to glorify God by whatever means He has gifted you to do so! That means, if you're gifted to clean, then clean as unto the Lord. If you're an encourager, encourage others as unto the Lord. If you can teach, preach, sing, speak, play music, write, draw- whatever it is may it be done as unto the Lord!

Matthew 5:16 says, "Let your light so shine before men, that they may see your good works, and glorify your Father which is in Heaven" (KJV). Live a life that is pleasing to God! Not men! According to Philippians 3:14 (KJV), we "press towards the mark for the prize of the high calling of God in Christ Jesus." Our mission is to spread the Gospel of Jesus Christ and win the lost souls to advance His Kingdom! We are commissioned in Matthew 28:19 to "Go and make disciples of all the nations, baptizing them in the name of the Father and the Son and the Holy Spirit."

Reproducing is not competition to see who can transform the most lives for Christ, or to see how many friends we can make, or how close we can get people to us in the process. It's about getting souls close to God! The glory in becoming a butterfly is emerging, spreading your wings, flying, and reproducing for God's glory! The cross I carried and the pain I endured was not punishment, but preparation for my greater. It was never about me or even for me, instead it was for you and for others reading this book who will forever be changed! Which brings me to the most crucial point in this book. Some of you may or may not know Jesus Christ as your personal Lord and Savior. If you don't know Him and would like to invite Him into your heart right now, please pray these words with me:

"Dear God,

I am a sinner who needs a Savior. I acknowledge that Jesus Christ is Lord. Forgive me for my sins, I believe your word is true! I believe in my heart and I confess with my mouth that according to the scriptures, Jesus was born of a virgin, He lived a sinless life, He died for my sins, and was resurrected on the third day for my justification. Jesus, come into my heart, let your Holy Spirit reign, rule, and abide in me. I am a new creature in Christ! Old things are passed away; behold all things are becoming new! Help me to do your will forever more! In Jesus' name I pray, Amen."

I believe that God heard you! He hears your prayers and He knows your heart. Always remember the cost and the cause of the Cross. The cross Jesus carried cost Him his life, He endured much affliction, He suffered and died. He became broken so that you and I could be made whole. This sacrifice was for our freedom and for our salvation. Perhaps moving forward, you'll see your pain in a different light and you'll carry your cross for the next person with Christ in mind.

Closure

A door finally closed that I once strived to keep open. A stiffness released that once could not be dismissed. A breath of relief that I once could not take, a tear finally drops that I once could not break.

A memory vanished that I once could not forget; silhouette's fading that I once failed to forget. A feeling I once felt is now replaced, a person I used to know now has no face. A dream I once lost has now been found, a voice I could not perceive now has a clear sound. An empty space in my heart is now filled and beats to its own rhythm; a love I once prayed for is now evolving.

A certain stillness I desired has finally come my way, to free me of the heartache and bring light to my day. I've longed for the moment when closure knows my name; when healing brings about contentment and leaves behind all the pain.

Closure happens when something is complete, at long last, I am healed. I am set free!

In the end… I treasure the pain.

Conclusion

A butterfly never forgets that it was once a caterpillar. The beauty in being transformed is realizing that I wouldn't be the woman I am today without being the person I was yesterday. Every struggle in my life thus far-from wrestling with my uniqueness as a child to completely losing my identity through the pain I endured was necessary. If I hadn't gone through it, I wouldn't have the compassion, empathy, or desire to help set others free! I'm so glad that God doesn't rest for our sake until we are free from bondage!

I have a lot more living to do, if it's God's will. In no way have I "arrived", but I do know the direction in which I'm going. I am called and equipped by God to heal, deliver, and transform lives beautifully for Christ. My scars no longer remind me of my inadequacy, but my purpose. My scars are proof that God heals. I've accepted that if I needed my natural womb to fulfill my destiny, then I wouldn't have lost it. And if God wants to perform a miracle in my life, I have the faith to receive it.

My loss was the means through which I stumbled into my calling. Beautiful butterfly, I encourage you to let go of whatever is hindering your healing. Seek God's face and let Him erase every label inscribed on your heart that doesn't define you. Remove the mask because it's NOT who you are, you know who you are and whose you are! You are marked by God. A child of the King and your Heavenly Father delights in you! It's time to exchange your ashes for a crown of glory. No longer are you desolate, barren, undeserving, unfit, worthless, hopeless, powerless, or fruitless! You are beautiful, powerful, worthy, deserving, empowered, fruitful, productive, wanted, loved and you are more than enough! I pray that you have gained the strength to fight through your own transformation and that you'll one day have the courage to boldly share your testimony with others. Remember that God loves you and me both! If He did it for me, He can most certainly do it for you! Just trust Him.

List of References

1. "Butterfly Life Cycle/Butterfly Metamorphosis."
Learnaboutnature.com, www.thebutterflysite.com.

2. Wilson, Tracy V. "How Caterpillars Work." HowStuffWorks, 28
Apr. 2008, animals.howstuffworks.com/insects/caterpillar3.htm.

www.ingramcontent.com/pod-product-compliance
Lightning Source LLC
Chambersburg PA
CBHW071433090426
42737CB00011B/1646